Understanding

Beulah Tannenbaum
Myra Stillman

Sound

illustrated by Adolph Brotman and with photographs

McGraw-Hill Book Company

New York · St. Louis · San Francisco · Düsseldorf
Johannesburg · Kuala Lumpur · London · Mexico
Montreal · New Delhi · Panama · Rio de Janeiro
Singapore · Sydney · Toronto

Contents

To the Reader

Throughout this book, you will find many suggested investigations that you yourself can try. They are included in the body of the text and easy to find because their first few words are set in all capitals. You do not need special equipment for these investigations. Usually you can find what you need around your home or you can buy the items in a dime store. We suggest that you try as many of these investigations as possible. They will add to your enjoyment of the book.

CREATING SOUND

Sounds

1

Your ears are never free from sounds. Day and night, a variety of sounds beat against your eardrums. Some you like: the referee's whistle beginning a ball game, the music of your favorite records. Some you dislike: the screech of chalk against the board, the squeal of a car as the driver jams on the brakes. Sometimes you wish all sound could be stopped so that there would be complete silence.

Astronauts walking on the moon could have experienced such silence if they did not use the communications systems in their spacesuits; there is no sound on the moon. On earth, silence is more difficult to find; except in soundproof chambers, there are sounds around us at all times. *Acoustics* is the science that deals with sound, and scientists speak of the sounds that always surround us as the *acoustical environment*. This environment can be made pleasant with welcome sounds, and it can be polluted by unnecessary noise—unpleasant sounds.

Man-made soundproof chambers can approach, but not quite reach absolute silence—the complete absence of sound. What is it like when the chamber door is closed and the din of the usual acoustical environment suddenly ceases? No one really seems to like the experience. Some people feel as if their ears are about to explode. Others are sure that they hear a humming sound that seems to come from within their own bodies.

Sounds made within the chamber are greatly magnified. The slightest movement makes your clothes swish and rustle. You do not ordinarily hear the sound of writing with a ballpoint pen, but in a soundproof chamber, even on the smoothest paper, the pen scratches loudly while the paper crackles menacingly. An acoustical environment without sound is strange, and the human body reacts with alarm to the strangeness, which seems oppressive.

In the normal world around us, there is a continuous background of sound, broken occasionally by sudden or different sounds that attract our attention. Most of the time, we do not notice the background sounds; sometimes we are even unaware that they exist. A camper in Death Valley may think he is in a soundless environment, yet if he strains, he can catch the faint whisper of the wind in the background. But we also become accustomed to very loud background noises. A camper on an ocean beach can become unaware of the constant pounding surf. However, either camper would hear an unexpected footstep on the sand.

Background sounds can tell us many things when we choose to listen to them. If you waken in a dark room, the sounds can provide clues as to where you are and even the approximate time. Some sounds are characteristic of particular places. For example, in a big city, you can hear the rumble of the traffic. In the country, you may hear the insects, or the night-prowling animals, or the flowing water in a mountain stream. Some sounds are commonplace at different times of the day or night. The city traffic is generally less noisy after midnight. At dawn in the country, the birds begin to sing and the cock crows.

Sit very still where you are now, and listen carefully. Do the sounds tell you things about the world around you which your eyes cannot see? The next time you ride in a car or in the school bus, close your eyes, and after a short period of time, try to determine from the sounds you hear where along its route the bus or car is.

Most animals depend on sound as an "early warning system," and man is no exception. Stealthy footsteps, growling dogs, even changes in the tone of a voice put us on guard. Cars are equipped with horns, trains with whistles or horns or bells, and emergency vehicles with sirens, not because each does not make a noise by itself, but because their noises tend to blend into the background sounds. Sudden, sharply different sound is needed to attract immediate attention and warn of danger. In the past, horse-drawn sleighs had bells on them because pedestrians often would not notice the swish of the runners or the soft clop of the horses' hooves striking the snow-covered road.

Even while we sleep, the sense of hearing protects us. Not only will we waken to a loud scream in the night, but the absence of usual background sounds will alert a sleeper. A man napping during a television sportscast, complete with pounding horses, a screaming announcer, and cheering fans, will waken if the television set is turned off and the loud but familiar background sounds cease.

What is sound that it can cause us to react whether we are awake or asleep? What is the first thing that comes into your mind when you hear the word *sound?* Do other people have the same reaction when they hear the word? Ask some of your friends to respond instantly when you say the word *sound*. Even if the answers differ slightly, you and your friends share the same meaning of the word. Yet the word itself is no more musical nor noisy than other words you know and use.

The word *sound* is part of a code that carries meaning to the brain of a person who understands English. Other languages use different words to convey the same meaning. For Spanish-speaking people, the word is *sonido*. The people of Africa who speak Swahili say the word *sauti*. In Japan, the word is 音 (oto). And if you were Russian, the word would be $zbyk$ (zvook). When you learn another language, you are really learning the code which the people who speak that language use to communicate with each other.

Whatever language they use, scientists define sound in the same way. Sound, they say, is "a mechanical disturbance in an elastic medium." This definition of sound can be memorized easily, but it may be meaningless until you know the answers to such questions as: How is sound made? How does sound travel? What happens to things, including the human body, that are in the path of sound?

Making Sounds
2

Suppose you sat next to a stranger on a bus. You discussed the weather briefly. Then the stranger told you in which part of your home state you grew up, and he also named another place where you had lived for at least a year. What would you think? Would you wonder if perhaps the stranger were a member of the F.B.I.? Or would you think that by some coincidence a friend had told him about you? You might begin to wonder whether it was magic, or you could just decide that it was a good guess. It is most likely, however, that the stranger is a speech expert, and the few comments you made about the weather told him all he needed to know. It was not the meaning of the words that gave him his clue, but the sound of those words as you spoke them. The way you said the words told him where you had lived.

You too may use this device to tell you something about people. From listening to them talk, you can probably recognize people who come from the South, or from New England, or from the West. Perhaps you have noticed that people who come from other countries and who learned to speak English as adults sound a little strange, even though they use the correct words and the correct grammar. They may have lived next door to you for many years, and still you can hear a difference. Even without being told, you may be able to guess the language they spoke as children. This difference in the sound of the spoken language is called an *accent*.

It is highly probable that as you learn to speak another language, you will speak that language with an American accent. People who live where that language is commonly spoken will recognize that you come from another place. Yet children who grow up in bilingual homes (homes where two languages are commonly used) and children from multilingual homes (homes where more than two languages are used) usually learn to speak each of the languages without an accent. What causes an accent, and why is it so difficult to get rid of one?

The problem is not that people cannot make the correct sounds, but that the human voice can make so many different sounds. The human voice mechanism is capable of making hundreds of sounds. Each word you speak is made up of several sounds. There are five sounds in the word *sounds*. Say the word slowly. Can you hear each of the five sounds? If all the sounds that can be made by the human voice were combined in all the possible ways, a person could start talking the moment he was born, talk continuously day and night for all the years of his life, and never repeat a word.

Out of the possible sounds, men have constructed over 6,000 different languages and *dialects*. A dialect is a form of a language which differs in pronunciation and expressions from *those used by* most people who speak the language. Different languages and dialects use different sounds, but each dialect uses only a small number of the possible sounds. In any one dialect of American speech, only between forty and forty-five sounds are combined in different ways to make up a vocabulary of about a million words. Because only a few of the sounds are used differently, you probably can tell whether someone who lives on the east coast comes from Brooklyn or from the Boston area, and you have no difficulty understanding him. However, in some countries, different dialects of the same language use many totally different sounds. In those countries, people who come from different sections and speak different dialects cannot understand each other's speech but they have no difficulty understanding each other's writing.

People talk so much and so easily that they think talking is simple; actually it is a very complicated process. A baby makes all kinds of sounds, but as he learns to talk, he uses only the sounds of the language that he hears spoken around him. He uses these sounds over and over, and his speech mechanism learns to reproduce the sounds exactly. He does not have to think about how to make the sounds; it becomes automatic. This is fortunate because of all the things you must do and all the parts of your body that are involved when you talk, even when you just say two words to greet a friend.

First in action is your brain. It fits securely in the small case called a skull. The brain weighs only about one and one-half pounds, but can outperform a massive computer. You spot your friend across the street. Your brain takes electrical signals called *impulses* that travel along the optic nerves from your eyes, compares these impulses with information stored in your memory, and then sends out other electrical impulses to the muscles which control the movements of your lungs, larynx, palate, tongue, jaw, and lips. Each of these parts of your body responds to the instruc-

13

tions from your brain by performing very exact movements, and you say, "Hello, Tom," or "Jane."

The many parts of the body that are used for speech perform more vital functions first. The work of the brain extends far beyond producing and receiving sounds. The lungs are where speech begins, but the more important task of the lungs is providing a continuous source of oxygen for the blood and expelling carbon dioxide from the body. The mouth and throat are essential for eating and also allow for the passage of gases to and from the lungs. Teeth are necessary for the chewing of food, while the tongue assists the swallowing of food and serves the sense of taste. The nose allows air to enter and leave the body and is involved in the sense of smell. If you think you do not use your nose when you speak, HOLD YOUR NOSTRILS closed and try to say "singing."

It has been said that if an inventor started out to design a single machine to serve so many different and unrelated purposes, people would laugh him out of existence. Yet, by using his multipurpose organs, man can make intelligible sounds and communicate with other men.

The job of the lungs as part of the human voice is to put air in motion. HOLD A STRIP of facial tissue about one inch wide in front of your mouth. Open your mouth slightly and inhale; the tissue will move toward your lips. Exhale, and the tissue will move away. Now try saying any group of English words. Watch the tissue and observe whether you inhale or exhale each time you say a word. Try to say the same word using first exhaled and then inhaled breath.

Most of the speech sounds of the major languages of the world use exhaled breath. All English words are said with exhaled breath, but there are languages which use inhaled air for forming sounds. In Khoisan, spoken by the Hottentots and Bushmen of Africa, inhaled air is used to produce the clicking sounds which are a part of the language. What do you suppose would happen if you learned to speak a language which includes inhaled sounds? Do you think you might often forget and use exhaled air instead? If you did, it would certainly sound as if you were speaking the language with an accent. And, if no one ever told you that you were supposed to inhale, you might never learn to make the sounds correctly, no matter how hard you tried. But many actors, who have studied how sounds are made, can learn to imitate a foreign dialect almost exactly. Perhaps a few could even fool the speech expert you met on the bus.

By themselves, the lungs do not make sound. You can breathe out silently, but if you place a whistle in your mouth and hold your nose, sound will be made as you exhale. Obviously, the whistle must do something to change the stream of air set in motion by your lungs.

Look at a police, scout, or athletic-type whistle. The stream of air which enters the mouthpiece is pushed into a rounded section or cavity. There is no opening opposite the mouthpiece slit through which the air enters the cavity, and so the air cannot continue straight ahead. The moving air, which you exhale or blow into the mouthpiece, bounces off the wall of the cavity, and eventually finds its way out through the opening on the upper side of the cavity. But the forward direction of the moving air has been disturbed. The whistle has created a disturbance in the stream of air. It is this disturbance in the stream of air which you hear as the sound of the whistle.

YOU CAN FIND out the effect of the small round

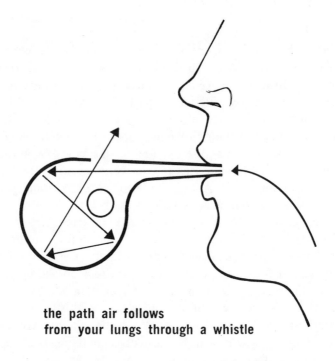

**the path air follows
from your lungs through a whistle**

cork or plastic ball that can be found in most whistles of
this type. Carefully spear the cork with a long pin or
needle. Hold the cork motionless while you blow the
whistle. (If your whistle has a hard plastic ball, use a
toothpick to keep it motionless.) Also, try holding the cork
in different positions within the cavity (next to the mouthpiece, against the side opening, and so on) to find out if
the position of the cork affects the sound of the whistle.

If the whistle you have is a penny whistle or party horn-
type, the mouthpiece is partly blocked, and the air must
pass between two pieces of metal. The rounded piece of
metal is rigid. It will not bend if you push it with a needle
or pencil point. But, try pushing against the straight piece

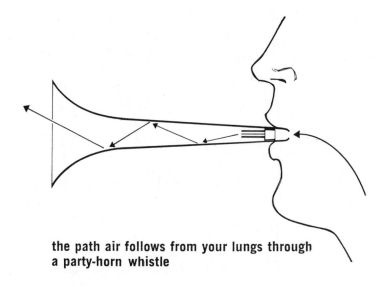

the path air follows from your lungs through a party-horn whistle

of metal. Notice how easily it moves back and forth; it is flexible. When you blow through the mouthpiece, the stream of air is squeezed between the two pieces of metal as it travels toward the bottom of the horn. The squeezed air pushes hard against the edge of the flexible metal strip, making it *vibrate*—move back and forth. In turn, the vibrating strip of metal pushes back against the air and creates a disturbance in it. The sound you hear is caused by the disturbance in the stream of air which leaves the horn.

YOU CAN MAKE another kind of whistle simply by using a blade of grass about three inches long or a strip of paper three inches long by one-fourth inch wide. Hold the grass or paper tightly and securely between your thumbs as shown in the picture. Place your mouth against your thumbs and blow hard against the edge of the grass or paper. The grass or paper strip, like the metal strip in the party whistle, is flexible. It can move back and forth easily.

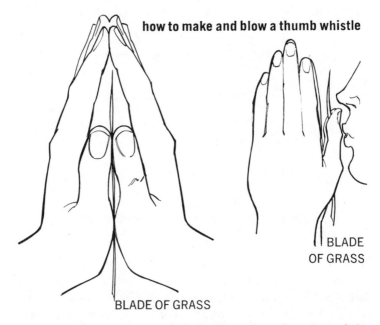

how to make and blow a thumb whistle

BLADE
OF GRASS

BLADE OF GRASS

As you blow a stream of air hard against the edge of the paper or grass, the flexible strip vibrates rapidly. You can feel the movement as a tickling sensation against your lips. The moving grass or paper tickles your lips and also creates a disturbance in the stream of air passing between your thumbs. You hear the disturbance as sound.

If you could slow down the movement of the vibrating paper or grass, this is what you would see: the vibrating body would move back and forth about the same distance in each direction at regular intervals of time. The motion might make you think of the moving pendulum of a clock or of a swing. Both of these are vibrating bodies, but because they move so slowly, you do not hear the disturbances created in the air by their vibrations.

18

When you speak, disturbances in the stream of air coming from your lungs are created in the *larynx*. The larynx or *voice box* is located toward the front of the throat. Within the larynx, there are two small sensitive ligaments called the *vocal cords*. The cords can vibrate, and so their function can be compared to that of the grass or paper strip in the thumb whistle. The stream of air flowing from the lungs sets the cords in motion and the motion of the cords disturbs the flowing air.

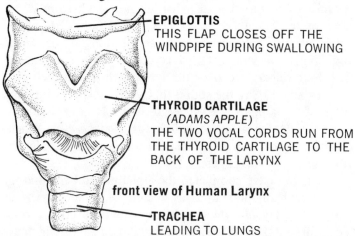

EPIGLOTTIS
THIS FLAP CLOSES OFF THE
WINDPIPE DURING SWALLOWING

THYROID CARTILAGE
(ADAMS APPLE)
THE TWO VOCAL CORDS RUN FROM
THE THYROID CARTILAGE TO THE
BACK OF THE LARYNX

front view of Human Larynx

TRACHEA
LEADING TO LUNGS

If you go back to your thumb whistle, YOU WILL FIND that you can change the sound of the whistle in two ways. First, you can press your thumbs more tightly together to change the size of the opening through which the stream of air must be squeezed. If you can close the opening completely, no sound will occur. If the opening is too large, no whistle will be produced. Second, you can hold the strip a little more tightly or a little more loosely to change the *tension* on the strip, and thus affect the way it vibrates.

19

The vocal cords too can be adjusted to change the sounds produced. First, the cords can move toward or away from each other, thus changing the size of the opening through which the air must be squeezed. No sound is produced when the cords are tight together or when the cords are completely opened. The latter is the position during normal breathing. Second, the cords can stretch and contract, thus becoming tighter or looser. This change in tension also affects the sound produced.

Only a few sounds in English do not result from vibrations of the vocal cords. YOU CAN DISCOVER which letters of the alphabet do not use vibrating cords. Place your fingers on your neck over your larynx. (You can tell that your fingers are over the larynx when you feel your Adam's apple.) Say the sound that you associate with each letter of the alphabet. Exaggerate or prolong each sound. For example, for *A* say *ahahahah,* for *B* say *beeeeee.* Whenever your cords vibrate to make a sound, you will feel the vibrations in your fingers.

When you have completed the alphabet, go back and try to sing each of the sounds as you make it. Sing the *A* as ycu would say *ah* when a doctor examines your throat. You will find that you can sing only those sounds which are created when your vocal cords vibrate. No matter how you try, you will not be able to sing some sounds such as the hiss of an *S* because the cords do not vibrate.

The vocal cords are called the "buzz source" of the sounds of the human voice. They create the raw buzz that is changed into words by other parts of the vocal tract. One strong buzz sound is the *M* sound. As you begin to hum an *M,* your vocal cords close. The air pushed against them by your lungs builds up pressure and forces its way between the vocal cords like an explosion. As soon as the pressure is reduced by the explosion, the cords come together again, close off the air passage, and again pressure builds up. The result is a series of rapid explosions, more than 100 each second. The vocal cords move back and forth swiftly with each explosion—they vibrate. Your fingers feel the series of explosions as vibrations of the local cords.

As each little explosion pops out from behind your vocal cords, the escaping air is compressed. Its molecules are squeezed closer together; they form a high-pressure area called a *crest*. Once past the vocal cords, there is room for the molecules to spread out. But in doing this, they push against and compress the molecules in the air ahead, and the crest advances. The molecules behind the crest are under somewhat less than normal pressure and so are part of a *trough,* or area of low pressure.

If the vocal cords opened and closed only once, a single pressure area would be formed and a single crest and trough would move forward through the mouth into the air beyond. However, the vocal cords open and close rapidly many times to make each sound. As a result, a series of high and low pressure areas or crests and troughs are formed. Such a series is called a *sound wave.*

Dots are used in the following diagrams to represent the molecules in the air. Remember that the sizes of the dots and the spaces between them as shown are not in the correct proportion. If air were magnified so that the molecules were the size of the dots in the diagrams, the average spaces between the molecules would be much greater than shown.

As a sound wave passes through air, water, or some other medium, it exerts pressure on the molecules, squeezing them together. But the molecules are not pushed on-

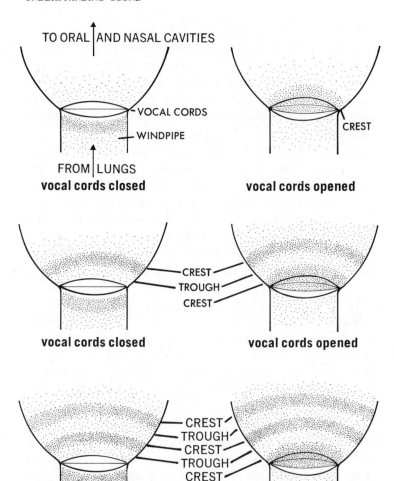

ward with the sound wave. As the crests advance, the molecules return to approximately the same position they were in before the sound wave reached them.

22

It would be very tiresome if every time one wished to il-
lustrate a sound wave, he was forced to use the dot method.
For convenience, the wave is usually shown as a curved
line. The high parts of the line, or crests of the wave, represent the high levels of pressure, and the low parts, or
troughs, represent the areas of reduced pressure. In such a
one-dimensional representation, a sound wave appears as if
it is traveling only in one direction. Actually, sound waves
move out in all directions around the source.

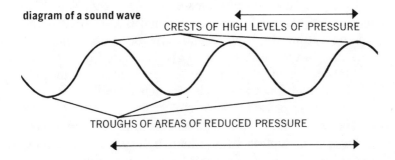

diagram of a sound wave

CRESTS OF HIGH LEVELS OF PRESSURE

TROUGHS OF AREAS OF REDUCED PRESSURE

By thinking of sound as a disturbance that causes a series
of high- and low-pressure areas in a material such as air—
the scientist's "mechanical disturbance in an elastic
medium"—it is EASY TO SEE why a vibrating body creates sound. Stretch a small rubber band between your
thumb and forefinger. Watch the movement of the band as
you pluck one side. You can see the band move back and
forth, or vibrate. Each time it moves forward it compresses
the air ahead, and each time it moves back, the band leaves
an area of less than normal pressure. You hear the alternat-
ing areas of high and low pressure as the characteristically
soft pinging sound of a stretched rubber band.

The sounds of all stringed instruments are created in a similar fashion. They may be caused by the pluck of fingers on a guitar string, the drawing of a bow across a violin string, or the mechanical hammer striking a piano wire. In every case, something starts the string vibrating. Something imparts motion, which is one form of *energy,* to the string. The string, in turn, transmits the energy by disturbing, placing in motion, the air around it. This disturbed air causes the motion energy to go onward through the surrounding air.

Energy is necessary to create sound. Light, heat, and motion are forms of energy, but sound is not usually considered a form of energy. Sound is the disturbance that occurs in a substance when energy is transferred through the substance. Sound is a result of energy (motion) from a vibrating body being transferred, through a substance such as air, from one place to another place.

The energy source for most wind instruments is a stream of air put in motion by the human lungs. The vibrating body, however, is not the same in each type of instrument. The clarinet, oboe, saxophone, English horn, and bassoon are called reed instruments because they use pieces of reed as vibrators. The reeds are shaved to produce thin edges. Air blown against these edges causes the reeds to vibrate the way the thin strip of metal vibrates when you blow into a party whistle.

For most brass instruments, such as the French horn and the trombone, the vibrating body is the lips of the musician. Beginning players of these instruments must learn the proper *embouchure,* the proper position of the mouth and lips. This is important so that when the player blows air into the instrument his lips are vibrating correctly to set up the exact disturbance in the air to produce the desired tone.

Flutes, piccolos, and some organ pipes depend on blowing air across the sharp edge of a hole. This causes vibrations in the air inside the instrument. This system of producing vibrations is somewhat similar to that of the police or athletic whistle.

One wind instrument which cannot depend on the lungs for its stream of air is the organ. Its pipes are too large to be blown by a human. However, the energy to operate old-fashioned organs did come from motion provided by the human body. Parlor organs were pumped by the feet. The foot pedals squeezed bellows, which supplied the streams of air to the pipes. The tremendous pipe organs in churches were pumped by hand, and often required several men or boys to provide sufficient energy. The huge organ which was built in Winchester Cathedral in England more than 1,000 years ago had 400 pipes and 26 bellows. It needed 2 players and 70 men to operate the bellows. At one time in America, pumping a church organ was considered a good way for a boy to earn money. Big pipe organs still depend on a moving stream of air, but boy power as an energy source has been replaced by electric blowers. Electric-powered organs should not be confused with modern, compact electronic organs that do not use pipes of air at all.

Another major group of musical instruments is the percussion instruments. Vibrations are set up in the instrument when it is struck, and energy is transmitted from a moving stick or hand. Drumheads usually are made of an elastic material such as animal skin. The skin is stretched very tightly over an opening, and energy is imparted to it by the striking stick or the beating hand. A few bits of light material, such as pieces of paper or dry cereal flakes placed on a drumhead, will dance in response to its vibrations, even when the head is tapped very gently.

When a triangle is struck, the entire triangle vibrates to create the sound. With cymbals, both halves of the instrument vibrate when they strike each other. If you touch the drumhead or any part of the triangle or cymbals with your hand, you will stop the vibrations, and the sound will cease immediately. Musicians call this *damping,* and they use it when the score indicates the end of the phrase.

Not all sound can be classed as music; much of it is just plain noise, which is often defined as loud, disagreeable, or unexpected sound. Like music, noise requires an energy source. Unlike music, which is a sequence of tones caused by different vibrations, noise may be only a single vibration. Clap your hands together sharply just once. Your hands have created a single vibration. The *shock wave* moves through the air in all directions. It affects the air in the same way as a single explosion popping between your vocal cords. However, most noise is created by more than one vibration. The shock wave of an explosion is usually followed by lesser sound waves caused by material near the center of the explosion which is also put into motion.

The motion of your hands as you clapped was the source of the energy which disturbed the air and made the sound. Not all of the energy of the motion was used to produce the shock wave. Some of the energy was transformed into heat. The next time you clap long and hard for a favorite performer, notice how hot the palms of your hands feel. In the case of chemical explosions, such as the detonation of dynamite, the energy was stored in the chemical substances involved. The energy is released suddenly as the result of a chemical reaction. Again, heat and even light may be

26

produced as well as the motion which creates the noise.

Heat energy from a stove can be turned into motion energy which can cause sound. Heat applied to the molecules in the water in a kettle causes the molecules to move faster and faster. The rapidly moving molecules escape from the liquid as a gas and push out through a small hole, setting the kettle whistle vibrating. The vibrating whistle sets up the sound waves that loudly announce that the kettle is boiling.

Steam whistles were once a part of the fun and work worlds of the American people. The warning whistles of the old locomotives were steam operated. Most factories announced the noon hour as well as the opening and closing of the day's work with loud blasts of steam whistles. These steam whistles were practical because the locomotives and the factory machines were driven by steam.

No traveling circus or showboat was complete without a steam calliope, which is sometimes called a steam organ since its sounds are produced by vibrating steam in its pipes instead of air. Even today, the last float of every presidential inaugural parade carries an old-fashioned steam calliope.

Differences in Sound Waves

3

Bands playing parade music, babies crying, students cheering at a football game, girls whispering secrets, sirens wailing, teachers speaking, two friends calling to each other across a busy street—think about the many sounds you hear. Obviously, the sound waves that reach you from these various sources must differ from each other. The shrill police whistle certainly must create a disturbance in the air different from the deep moan of a foghorn. When someone sings softly to himself, he must affect the air around him differently from when he sings the same song as a concert solo in a large auditorium.

One way sound waves differ is in *intensity* or *power:* how much energy the sound wave transmits. Intensity is related to loudness. Sing a note softly, and then sing the same note louder and louder. You can feel yourself making a greater effort, using more and more power. By the time you are singing the note as loud as you can, you probably feel that you are using a tremendous amount of power to put forth all that energy to create the sound wave.

Since sound travels out in all directions from the source, the energy is spread over larger and larger areas. The closer to the source of a sound you are, the more intense the

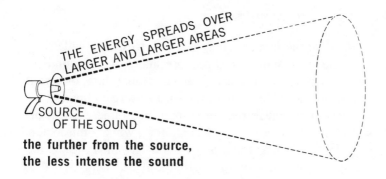

THE ENERGY SPREADS OVER LARGER AND LARGER AREAS

SOURCE
OF THE SOUND

**the further from the source,
the less intense the sound**

sound is. The farther away from a source you are, the less sound power reaches you.

Sound power is usually measured in *watts per square meter*. The watt was named in honor of James Watt, the Scottish instrument maker who perfected the steam engine. Watt needed a standard for measuring the power (the rate of doing work) of his steam engines. So he found out how much work a strong horse could do in one second, and then used *horsepower* to measure the energy output of his engines. In the metric system, watts are used instead of horsepower. One horsepower equals 746 watts. Watts are also used to measure energy output in electricity. Many light bulbs in your home probably were designed for 100 watts.

A source of sound with a power of 100 watts placed 1 meter from your ear would make you feel extreme pain. Even a source of 10 watts at the same distance would cause an annoying sensation as well as an unbearably loud sound. At the same distance, 1 meter, you probably could just barely hear a sound created by a source with a power of about .0000000001 (1 ten billionth) watt. If your eyes were as sensitive as your ears, you would be able to see light from a 100-watt bulb shining 2,000 miles away.

Because the human ear is sensitive to such a wide range of intensity of sound, and because many of the sounds we hear are measured in very small fractional parts of a watt, the watt is not a convenient unit of measure. Instead, intensity is usually measured by comparing sounds. Thus, one sound may be twice as loud as another, while a third sound may be 10 times as loud. Scientists determined the smallest change in intensity of sound that can be distinguished by the normal human ear and used it as the unit for measuring intensity. It is called 1 *decibel* (*db*). A decibel is $\frac{1}{10}$ of a *bel* (named for Alexander Graham Bell, a speech teacher and the inventor of the telephone).

The sound level at which the normal ear can just discern sound is arbitrarily called 0 (zero) decibel. The rustle of leaves in a light breeze is judged to be 10 times as great as the least sound a human can hear. It is rated at 10 db (1 bel). The decibel scale is not arithmetic, so that a sound of 20 db (2 bels) is not twice as loud as a 10-db sound. The decibel scale uses a logarithm base, so that a sound of 20 db is 10 times as loud as a 10-db sound. An average whisper 4 feet away from the hearer is about 20 db or 100 times as great as a 0-db sound. A noisy city street may have a rating of 80 db or 100,000,000 (one hundred million) times as loud as a barely audible sound.

Many sounds people make today are considered too loud for comfort. The decibel rating of two discotheques in San Francisco where rock music was being played was between 90 and 120 db or between 1 billion and 1 trillion times as great as 0 db. Large air compressors, used to operate pneumatic drills for digging, may put out 110 decibels of sound. Jet engines often produce 120 decibels. At this level, sound becomes painful. A testing machine has been made which

30

Sound Level Chart

DECIBEL	BEL	TYPE OF SOUND	TIMES AS LOUD AS 0 DB
0	0	THE LEAST SOUND HEARD BY A NORMAL HUMAN EAR	
10	1	THE RUSTLE OF LEAVES IN A LIGHT BREEZE	10
20	2	AN AVERAGE WHISPER 4 FEET AWAY FROM HEARER	100
30	3	BROADCASTING STUDIO WHEN NO PROGRAM IS IN PROGRESS	1,000
40	4	NIGHT NOISES IN A CITY	10,000
50	5	AVERAGE RESIDENCE	100,000
60	6	NORMAL CONVERSATION AT 3 FEET	1,000,000
70	7	AN ACCOUNTING OFFICE	10,000,000
80	8	A NOISY CITY STREET	100,000,000
90	9	A MODERATE DISCOTHEQUE	1,000,000,000
100	10	A FOOD BLENDER	10,000,000,000
110	11	A PNEUMATIC DRILL	100,000,000,000
120	12	A JET ENGINE	1,000,000,000,000

produces over 170 decibels. Exposure to the sound of this machine for even a moment would make you unconscious and would permanently destroy your hearing. (See Chapter 9.)

Intensity is not the only factor that affects the loudness of a sound. You might expect three sounds of equal intensity, originating at the same place, to sound equally loud. Strangely enough, this might not be so. If a woman was standing one meter away from you, her shrill voice, even though it transmitted the same amount of energy the same distance, might not sound as loud as a man's deep voice. And if a bat flying one meter from you uttered its cry at the same intensity, you probably would not even hear it.

If you could watch several different sound waves pass by, you would notice that the pressure crests moved along at the same speed in each wave, but that the distances between the crests of one wave differed from the distances between the crests of other waves; they would have different *wavelengths*.

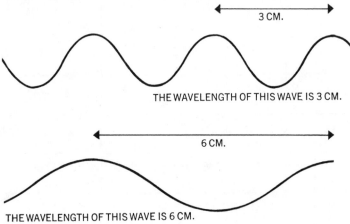

3 CM.

THE WAVELENGTH OF THIS WAVE IS 3 CM.

6 CM.

THE WAVELENGTH OF THIS WAVE IS 6 CM.

Since the speed of sound through any given medium is uniform if the crests are closer together (if the wavelength is shorter), the number of crests which pass any point during one second must be greater.

When an animal cries or a person speaks, many different sound waves are sent forth. If you could examine those made by a bat, most of the waves would show very short wavelengths. Most of the waves made by a woman would have somewhat longer distances between the crests, and the wavelengths of a man's voice would be longer still.

How often, or how frequently, a crest in a sound wave passes a given point is called the *frequency* of the sound wave. Frequency is measured in *cycles per second* (*cps*). A cycle is usually described as the part of a wave from one crest to the next. If you could count the number of pressure crests passing a given point in one second, that number would be the frequency of the wave.

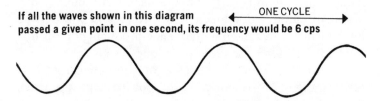

If all the waves shown in this diagram passed a given point in one second, its frequency would be 6 cps

ONE CYCLE

One cycle per second is also called 1 *hertz* (*Hz*) in honor of the German physicist Heinrich Rudolf Hertz. Hertz discovered radio waves (electromagnetic radiation) while studying the electromagnetic field around an electrical circuit. But he never lived to know how important his work was, nor did he ever hear a radio broadcast. He died of blood poisoning in 1894 at the age of thirty-seven.

If you could see every wave that a person with normal

hearing can hear through air, you would find that the shortest distance between pressure crests is just under 1 inch (2.5 centimeters), and the number of pressure crests that passed in 1 second would be about 20,000. If exactly 20,000 crests passed in 1 second, the frequency of the wave would be 20,000 cycles per second or 20 kilohertz (1,000 Hz = 1kHz). The longest wavelength people can generally hear is about 70 feet (about 20 meters). Such a wave has a frequency of only about 16 cps or 16 Hz.

Humans can generally hear sounds whose waves have frequencies between 16 cps and 20,000 cps. These are called *audible sound waves*. Animals other than man often have different ranges within which they can hear sound (see page 35), but the term audible is limited to frequencies which can be heard by humans.

Most people are more sensitive to sounds in the lower frequencies than to those in the higher frequencies, even though the intensity may be the same. Although many primitive cultures developed both drum- and whistle-type instruments, it was the low-frequency-producing drums that were used to send messages over long distances.

The use of drums as a means of communication may seem strange in the modern world, but it is still very much faster than the postal system. In a recent test, a team of drumbeaters in India picked up and relayed a message 300 miles in less than 20 minutes. Henry M. Stanley, the reporter who found Dr. David Livingstone in the jungles of Africa in 1871, relied on the local drum system of communication and felt it was as good as the telegraph which was already in wide use in many parts of the world.

The drum is made to talk by beating on different parts of the instrument. Each part vibrates differently. The rate at which the vibrating drum pushes against the air determines the wavelength and the frequency, and, therefore, the sound of the drum. Not only can skilled drumbeaters make a drum talk, they also can understand the drum language as readily as the spoken word.

If you could see every possible wave that can be produced, you would find some wavelengths even shorter than 2.5 centimeters, and other wavelengths greater than 20 meters. Sound waves in air with wavelengths of less than 2.5 centimeters and frequencies of more than 20 cps are usually called *ultrasonic,* but sometimes the older term *supersonic* is still used, though incorrectly. (Today, we should use the term supersonic only to describe speeds greater than the speed of sound.)

Even though the normal human ear cannot detect ultrasonic waves, they are used by a number of animals. You hear only part of a cricket's chirp; the higher frequencies are beyond your range of hearing. A bat, flying at night, can produce sounds up to 120,000 cps (120 kHz) to create the echoes which guide him. Dolphins, oil birds, sharks, and man-made sonar devices also use ultrasonic frequencies which pass unnoticed by human ears. But the fact that man cannot hear ultrasonic sounds does not limit their value to him. Man uses these frequencies to explore the world around him, and even to explore the inside of his own body (see pages 168–169).

Sound waves in air with pressure crests more than twenty meters apart and less than sixteen crests per second are called *infrasonic waves.* The sound spectrum extends down to less than one cycle per hour. In this low range are earthquake waves and other vibrations of the earth. Infrasound can set up vibrations in the human body that can cause

35

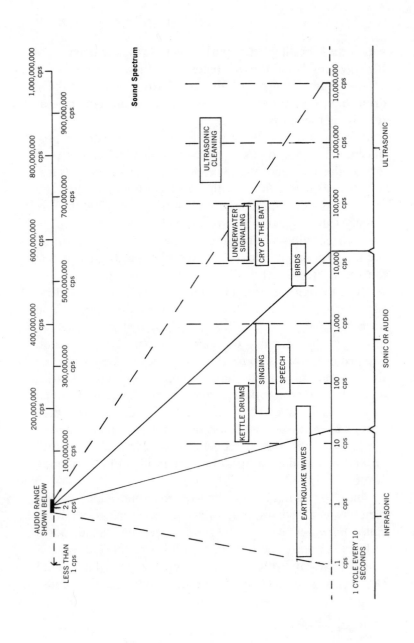

Sound Spectrum

quick death. At least one country, France, is investigating the practicality of an infransonic weapon. The following chart shows the ranges of some sounds, both audible and inaudible.

The frequency of a sound wave determines its *pitch:* how high or how low the sound is. YOU CAN DEMONSTRATE this relationship. Pucker your lips and blow out a steady stream of air as you count silently and slowly. Use your hand to cover and uncover your lips at each count. Listen carefully to the resulting sound. Now, try covering and uncovering your lips twice for every count, and then three times, and finally four times for each count. Notice the way the sound changes.

The siren-like instrument scientists use to study sound frequencies works in somewhat the same manner, except that it can move faster and has a steadier source of air. Instead of a hand moving over the lips, a disk with a series of holes is turned in front of a stream of air. When the disk moves slowly, you can hear a sound like the puff of an automobile exhaust each time a hole allows the stream of air to escape. When the disk is speeded up, the puffs or the crests of the sound waves occur more frequently; you hear a sound like a note played on a tuba or bassoon. If the disk is speeded up even more, the frequency of the sound wave created is increased, and the tone sounds as if it came from a clarinet. Faster still, the sound is like a tone from a flute, then a piccolo. And finally, if the disk is turned rapidly enough, you hear no sound at all, but your dog may howl in complaint against the rapid vibrations that are clearly audible to him.

If you look at the range of audible sound waves on the chart, you will notice that the sounds we think of as high-pitched are those with the shortest wavelengths and with the highest frequencies. The low-pitched sounds have the longest wavelengths and the lowest frequencies.

When you strike a key on a piano, a number of sound waves are produced, and not all have the same frequency. However, if you play the lowest key, it can produce sound waves with a distance of about 12 meters between pressure crests and 27.5 cycles will pass a given point in one second. When you play the highest key, the piano can produce a sound wave with a wavelength of only about 8 centimeters and a frequency of 4,186 cps. Middle C can produce a sound wave with a frequency of 261.6 cps. The frequency ranges of some other musical instruments are shown on the next chart.

Low-pitched sounds can be heard for greater distances than high-pitched sounds, and infransonic waves can travel further than ultrasonic waves. Ultrasonic waves rarely can travel more than a few feet from their source. But very low infransonic waves, such as those created in 1883 by the explosion of the East Indian volcano Krakatoa, can travel several times around the earth. Because ships at sea need plenty of space to change course so as to avoid danger, foghorns always are very low pitched to be sure their signals can be heard across miles of water. Low-frequency sounds can travel so far under water that someone once said that if there is ever a "shot heard 'round the world," it will be fired under water.

As sound waves are transmitted, some of the energy that created the disturbance is transformed into heat energy. The heat energy remains behind as the wave motion goes forward. In sound waves with high frequencies—waves which crest more often in one second—the original energy

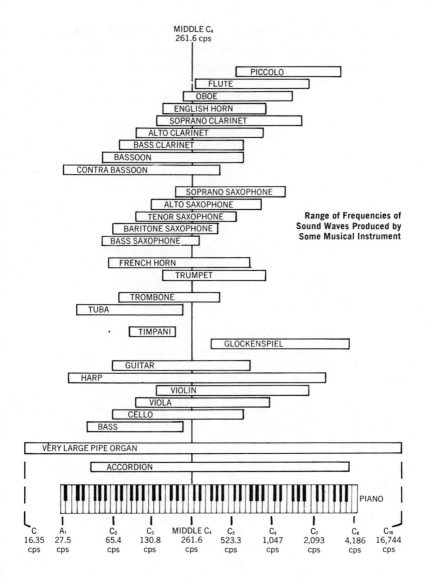

Range of Frequencies of Sound Waves Produced by Some Musical Instrument

is transformed into heat more rapidly than in waves with lower frequencies. This helps explain why a man's voice would sound louder than a higher-pitched woman's voice of the same intensity at the same distance (see page 32).

Shaping Sounds

4

People can hear a much wider range of sounds than they can produce with their voices. Human ears can hear sounds between about 16 cps and 20,000 cps, but the lowest note reached by a bass is F_1—about 48 cps, and the highest note reached by the phenomenal soprano Lucrezia Agujari, who lived in the eighteenth century, was C_7—2093 cps. Jenny Lind could only reach E_6—1320 cps. The range used in ordinary speech is much smaller, only about from 90 to 400 cps, and very few individuals can use that entire range. If you compare the human speaking range with the entire sound range, both audible and inaudible, human speech may seem rather insignificant. However, if you think about the fact that your brain can direct your voice mechanism to produce sounds of many different frequencies within this range, human speech becomes very impressive.

The frequency of the voice can be thought of as the number of "explosions" of air that escape from between the vocal cords each second (the cycles per second). An excited young child may produce as many as 400 explosions per second—a high-pitched sound. A man may average about 120 explosions per second in normal speech, while a woman's voice usually falls between the two, somewhere about

250 cycles per second. These differences in pitch are dependent on several factors including the length of the vocal cords. Among men, the length varies from 23 to 27 millimeters (about 1 inch). Women's vocal cords are usually shorter than men's.

The scientists at the Bell Telephone Laboratories are particularly interested in finding out how the sounds of the human voice are produced. They worked out a way to take moving pictures of the vocal cords in action. These pictures required an extremely fast camera and a series of mirrors, one of which was placed in the throat. When they slowed down the pictures, they could observe the action of the cords easily.

Even though it is impossible for most people to examine the workings of the human vocal cords, a comparison with

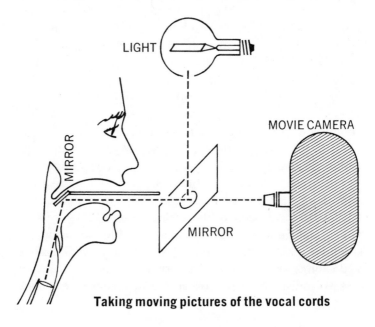

Taking moving pictures of the vocal cords

the strings of a guitar can be helpful in understanding how various voice frequencies can be produced. Each string of the guitar has a different thickness. The first string is the thinnest string, while the sixth string is the thickest. The strings are also called by the letters that correspond to the musical notes which they produce when *tuned*—when they vibrate at the most commonly used frequencies.

In 1955, an international commission decided that 440 cps should be the standard frequency for A_4 (A above middle C on the piano). Standardization was necessary so that a musical tone would have the same frequency when played by orchestras all over the world. Even in 1971, sixteen years after standardization, not all orchestras used the same pitch. For example, the Berlin Philharmonic used 449 cps, the Pittsburgh Symphony tuned to 442 cps, and the Russian orchestra preferred 435 cps. The standardized frequencies of all other musical tones are based on the A_4. Thus, middle C (C_4) becomes 261.6 cps and A_2 (the A of the guitar) becomes 110 cps.

When you pluck the first, thinnest, or E string, the string begins to vibrate rapidly. If the guitar is tuned, the vibrations will create sound waves with a frequency of about 329 cps. The second or B string is a little thicker than the E string. When plucked, the B string has a frequency of about 246 cps. The B string vibrates more slowly than the E string, and consequently its pitch is lower. By plucking each succeeding string, you will notice that the thicker the string, the lower the pitch. The thickness of the string is a factor in controlling the frequency of the resulting sound.

To change the pitch of any string, you must change the rate at which the string vibrates. One way to do this is to change the length of the string. The effective playing length of a guitar string can be shortened by placing a finger on

43

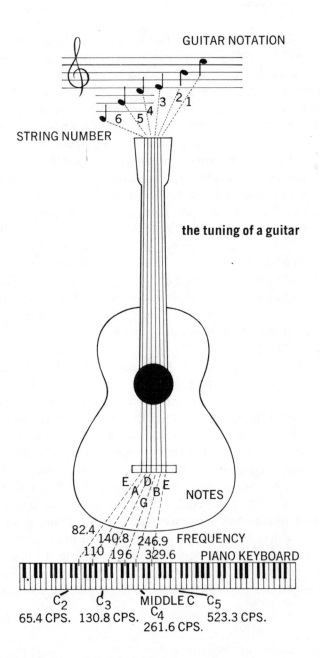

the tuning of a guitar

the string and holding it tightly against the fingerboard of the guitar. Then, when the string is plucked, only that part of the string between the bridge and the fret below the finger is free to vibrate. Thus the effective length is shortened; the string vibrates more rapidly.

If you place your finger over the first string, just above the first fret, the string will vibrate at about 349 cps, and the note played will be F rather than E. With your finger pressed against the third fret, the sound will have a frequency of about 392 cps, and the note will be G. As you move your finger down the fingerboard, you will find that

STRINGS

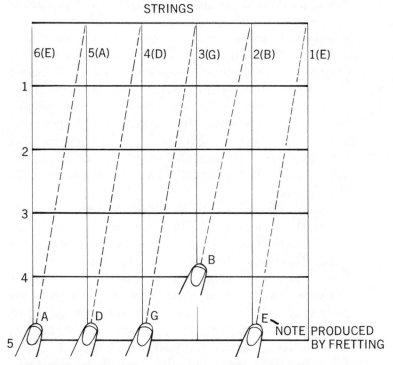

You can change the sound of a guitar by fretting it. The finger must press the string firmly against the fret

the shorter the effective length of the string, the more vibrations it makes per second and the higher is its pitch. The length of the vibrating string is a second factor that determines the frequency of sound.

If you hold your finger tightly against the second or B string just above the first fret, the sound will have a frequency of about 261 cps, and it will be a C. If you push your finger just above the third fret, the B string when plucked will produce a D. With a properly tuned guitar, you can make the sixth string vibrate at the frequency of an open fifth string by pressing your finger just above the fifth fret and plucking the string. The fifth string can be made to sound similar to the open fourth, and so on.

You cannot make any of the other strings sound similar to the open sixth string by fretting, since the open sixth string produces the guitar's lowest note. However, there is a way to make another string resemble the open sixth string. You can loosen one of the other strings, and then tighten it gradually until it produces the same note as the open sixth. *Tension,* how tightly the string is stretched, is a third factor in determining the frequency of sound. The tighter a given string is stretched, the higher becomes the frequency of the sound it makes.

Probably no two people have identical vocal cords, but in general, women and children have shorter and thinner vocal cords than men. Thus their voices are usually higher pitched. However, individuals have the ability to change the pitch of their voices somewhat by changing the tension of their vocal cords. Although the vocal cords are more like tightly stretched flaps than strings, the tension-changing relationships shown on the guitar strings apply to them. Thus, when you ask a question and your voice goes up at the end of it, your vocal cords have tightened in response to instructions from your brain. The tightened vocal cords produce sound with a higher frequency. When you drop your voice at the end of a statement, your vocal cords loosen. Changes in the pitch of your voice while speaking are called *inflections*. Without inflections, your voice would sound dull and monotonous, and some of the meaning of what you are saying might not be clear.

Not all languages use inflections in the same way. In Swedish, for example, every sentence ends on a rising inflection. A Swede may learn to pronounce and use English words perfectly, but if he does not change his native inflections, most people will say that he speaks with a Swedish accent.

The Chinese language makes an even greater use of inflections than English or Swedish. The meaning of a word may depend entirely on the inflection given it. Thus, in Chinese, the same utterance "ma" is used for both *mother* and *horse*. The meaning depends on a rising or falling inflection. Some language teachers think that learning new inflections is one of the most difficult parts of learning a new language.

When singing the voice uses a much greater frequency range than when talking. Normal singing-voice ranges are shown on the next chart. It is possible, with skilled voice training and practice, to increase the range of the singing voice by increasing the control over the vocal cords. This is one reason why famous singers continue to take singing lessons and to practice long hours each day. In a sense, they are learning to play their vocal cords as other musicians learn to play their instruments.

In discussing frequency, sounds have been treated as if they were pure tones. A pure or simple tone has a single pitch. However, except in experimental work, pure tones

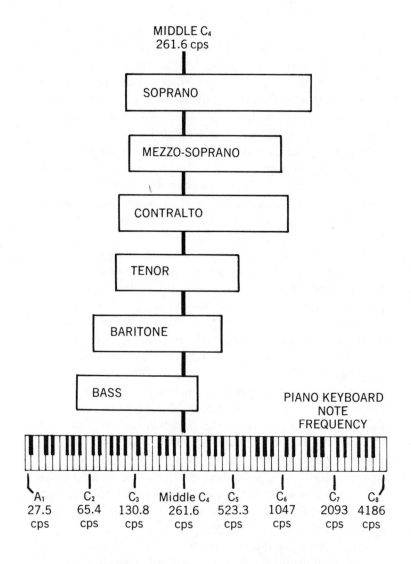

Approximate Ranges of Singing Voices

are rare. Most of the sounds we hear are composed of a number of sound waves, many of which have different frequencies.

Sounds are often classified either as noise or as musical tones. Sometimes noise is defined simply as unwanted sound. But a more technical description points out that noise is composed of sound waves of many frequencies distributed at random. That is, the frequencies do not necessarily have any regular or systematic relationship to each other. Sound which results from such a random combination of frequencies generally is not pleasing to the ear.

The sounds produced by musical instruments and the human vocal tract, however, do have definite mathematical relationships among the wave frequencies of which they are made. For example, when you strike the middle C key of a properly tuned piano, the *fundamental* or strongest part of the resulting sound will come from waves with a frequency of 261.6 cps. But, at the same time, the string will produce *overtones,* higher frequencies that are much fainter than the fundamental, but bear a mathematical relationship to it.

Overtones produced by stringed instruments result from an astonishing property of the strings. While the string is vibrating along its entire effective length to create the fundamental tone or frequency, it is, at the same time, vibrating in each of several fractional parts. Thus, the middle C string of the piano, while vibrating along its entire length to produce waves with a frequency of 261.6 cps, may also be vibrating as if it were two separate strings, each approximately half the length of the C_4 string. The waves created by these halves of the string are overtones and are called the first overtone or the second *harmonic*. When the string vibrates in three parts or thirds, it produces the second

49

A string can vibrate as a whole and in segments at the same time

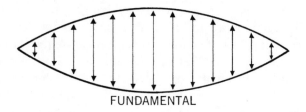

FUNDAMENTAL

FIRST OVERTONE
(*SECOND HARMONIC*)

SECOND OVERTONE
(*THIRD HARMONIC*)

overtone or third harmonic. Strings can produce third, fourth, fifth overtones, and so on.

The final composition of the note you hear played on a string instrument does not consist of equal parts of the overtones. The material from which the instrument is made reinforces some overtones, thus increasing their intensity. It absorbs other overtones, and so decreases their intensity.

50

Wind instruments also produce overtones or harmonics. In a wind instrument, the fundamental is determined by the vibration of the effective length of the column of air within the instrument. The overtones are caused by vibrations of fractions of this length. The lengths of the air columns of wind instruments like clarinets and flutes are regulated by opening and closing the holes in the walls of the instruments at various locations. The length of the effective air column in a trombone is increased and decreased by means of a slide. The problem is solved in a pipe organ by having a different size pipe for each note. In each case, the longer the air column, the lower the pitch of the note.

Whenever only a fraction of the air column is used for the fundamental, as in the upper registers of a flute, longer lengths of air can be set in vibration to produce *undertones* which are lower than the fundamental.

YOU CAN DEMONSTRATE the relationship between pitch and effective length of air column for yourself. You will need eight empty soda bottles and some water. Pull your lips tightly against your teeth and extend your upper jaw slightly beyond your lower jaw. In this position, you can blow downward. Hold the rim of an empty soda bottle against your lower lip and blow downward across it. Adjust the position of your lips and the position of the bottle until a clear musical tone is produced.

Pour a different amount of water into each of the seven other bottles. The water replaces some of the air, and so shortens the length of the air column in the bottle. The more water, the shorter the column of air. Blow across each of the bottles in turn. By adjusting the amount of water in each bottle, it is possible to produce a musical scale of one octave (eight related musical tones).

The fundamental wave frequency produced by disturbing

51

**how to produce a musical tone
with a soda bottle**

the air column in the bottle is usually accompanied by overtones. These overtones are caused by vibrations of fractional parts of the total air column. Since the overtones are caused by vibrations of a length of the column that is less than the total air column, the overtones have higher frequencies than the fundamental. If you blow across the bottle harder, in such a manner that only part of the air column creates the fundamental, the vibrations of longer lengths of air will produce undertones of lower frequencies. This is similar to using the upper register of a flute.

Certain overtones are characteristically produced by each type of musical instrument. Thus, the overtones of a given note on a clarinet differ from the overtones of that note when played by a flute. This difference in sound resulting from overtones of different frequency and intensity is called *quality*.

In addition to differences between different kinds of instruments, each instrument has a characteristic quality of its own. The makers of musical instruments try to control both the frequency and intensity of the overtones that will be produced by their instruments. They strive to produce overtones which create the most pleasant sound. One way to do this is to use certain materials. For example, a gold flute produces a more desirable sound than a silver flute, and a platinum flute is considered best by some musicians.

Skilled musicians can often identify a specific instrument by the quality of its tone. It is this quality, and not only the cost of the materials that account for the differences in value of musical instruments of the same type. Once the production of the most pleasant overtones was almost as much a matter of chance as of skill. Today, makers of musical instruments use computers to analyze the best musical instruments of the past and to design new instruments that are uniformly good in terms of their overtones.

The human voice tract also creates overtones as well as

fundamentals. Whereas the highest fundamental tone of a soprano is generally about 1,000 cps, the overtones extend the range to 3,500 cps or even higher. By emphasizing some of the overtones and suppressing others, our vocal tracts produce words. Words are shaped from raw sounds, the hissing, popping, and buzzing sounds that issue from between the vocal cords. The lips, tongue, palate, and oral and nasal cavities shape these sounds into intelligible words.

Probably everyone is aware that movements of the mouth are involved in speech, and most people also realize that the tongue plays a part. The exact movements that produce human speech have interested people for many centuries. As early as the first century B.C., a Greek who was teaching rhetoric in Rome published several books on the subject. He was Dionysius of Halicarnassus, in what is now Turkey. Dionysius sorted out a number of different sounds and described the tongue and lip positions necessary to produce them. He also understood the function of the lungs in speech.

Dionysius's work was original, but he was by no means the first to write about the production of the spoken word. Several centuries earlier, the scholars of India were faced with a problem. The hymns of the *Rig-Veda,* which is one part of the Brahman sacred scriptures, were first written down in Vedic, an ancient language. But by 400 B.C., Sanskrit had become the official language. The scholars realized that the correct pronunciation of the words of the hymns would in time be lost, so they set about studying the exact positions of the lips and tongue as each of the sounds in the words of the hymns was said. By describing these positions in the *Siksha,* a commentary written in Sanskrit, they hoped to ensure that the hymns would be properly intoned even when Vedic disappeared completely as a living language.

During the second half of the seventeenth century, Dr. John Wilkins, an Englishman, devised a method of showing the lip and tongue positions by schematic drawings. These were very complicated and not practical. About one hundred years later in the 1860s, Alexander Melville Bell, the father of Alexander Graham Bell, worked out a system which he called "visible speech." This consisted of a series of diagrams that represented mouth positions for various sounds. The elder Bell and his son became so adept at reading this visible speech that they could easily read each others notes drawn in this form. Bell's visible speech even included diagrams for yawns and hiccups.

For three generations in Scotland, the Bell family had studied the mechanics of sound. Alexander Graham Bell worked with his father, who was a pioneer in teaching speech to the deaf. After the family emigrated to the United States, Alexander Graham became professor of vocal physiology at Boston University. There, he fell in love with and married one of his deaf pupils. Because his wife Mabel's deafness was the result of a childhood illness, Bell's interest in educating deaf children became even greater. It was he who examined Helen Keller who had become blind and deaf at the age of eighteen months, and recommended the tutoring that made it possible for her to overcome her handicaps.

The movements of the tongue and lips in shaping words are readily available for research by anyone possessed of patience and a mirror. SAY THE VOWEL sounds as you watch the movement of your lips in the mirror. At the same

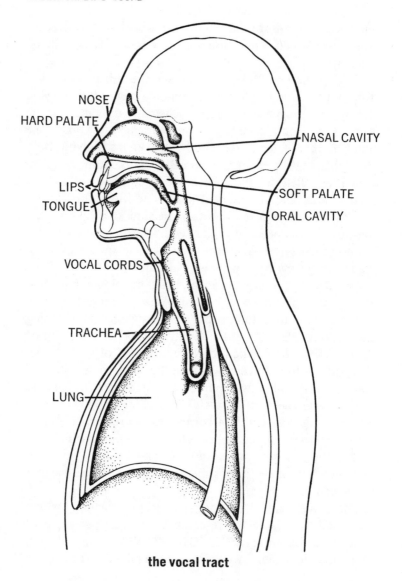

the vocal tract

time, be aware of the position of your tongue. Then try the sounds of the consonants. *M* and *N* have certain similarities when written. Do you find similarities in lip and tongue positions when you say these letters or when you make their characteristic sounds?

Do you remember what happened when you tried to say the word "singing" while holding your nostrils closed? Now, try saying a series of words. Find out which words will be distorted by this action and which will remain unchanged.

YOU CAN ALSO OBSERVE some of the effects of changing the shape of the oral cavity if you have an old hollow ball, such as a tennis ball, and a small whistle. Cut a slit in one side of the ball. The slit should be as small as possible and still permit the entrance of the whistle. The mouthpiece of the whistle should remain outside the ball. Blow on the whistle as you squeeze the ball to reshape the

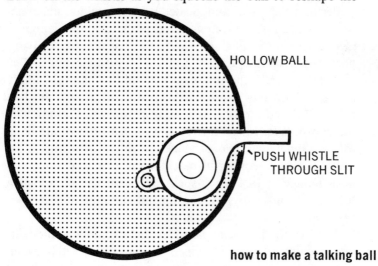

HOLLOW BALL

PUSH WHISTLE THROUGH SLIT

how to make a talking ball

cavity within the ball. If you blow steadily and squeeze the ball twice, quickly, you can produce a sound that resembles "ma-ma." If you slit the ball open on the side opposite from the whistle, you can hear what happens to the sound you produce as you open and close these "lips."

Your ball and whistle are a very crude form of "talking machine." The inventions of machines that would reproduce human speech were favorite projects during the eighteenth century. A Professor Kratzenstein invented such a machine and won a prize from the Russian Imperial Academy. He designed a series of tubes shaped to imitate the interior of the human mouth while making certain sounds. By using a reed which was set in vibration by a bellows, he could produce certain vowel sounds. About the same time, Abbé Mical in Paris and Wolfgang von Kempelen in Hungary built machines that could say words and even sentences.

Perhaps the most complicated of the speaking machines was produced about one hundred years later in Vienna by Herr Faber. This machine had for its vocal cords an ivory reed which could produce sounds of variable pitch. The size and shape of the oral cavity could be changed rapidly by depressing the keys of a keyboard. The machine had rubber lips and a rubber tongue to permit the formation of the consonants. In the throat there was a little windmill so that the machine could produce the rolling R sound. Herr Faber took his wonderful machine on tour, and whenever he exhibited it in French-speaking countries, he added a tube to its nose to produce the nasal tones of a proper French accent.

Some of the problems faced by the inventors of the talking machines can be imagined if you consider that when you speak rapidly, you may change the shape of your vocal tract as often as thirty times in one second. The invention of a satisfactory "talking machine" had to wait for the work of Thomas Edison who used the human ear as his model rather than the human vocal tract (see page 133).

As a result of modern technology, visible speech has reappeared as a method for studying sound. Computers can produce a 30-foot analysis of the sounds in a one-syllable word. Such an analysis shows the frequency and intensity of each sound that makes up the word. *Sound spectrograms* and the *voiceprints* made from them give us pictures of words as spoken by different people. Spectrograms are graphs of the intensities and frequencies of sounds and also the length of time each sound lasts. On a voiceprint, contour lines are drawn to connect sounds of equal intensity.

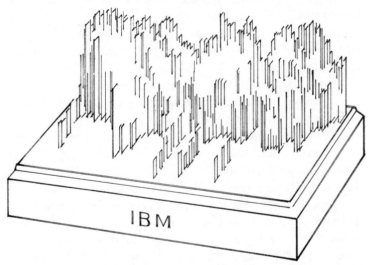

A 3-dimensional model of The Word "IBM"

Three-dimensional representations of words have also been made from spectrograms.

Because of this modern visible speech work, we now recognize that no two people speak alike even when they attempt to imitate each other. The imitation may deceive the human ear, but the voiceprint can show the differences. Voiceprints also show differences in the speech of the same person at different times.

Voiceprints are now being put to practical use. Visible speech has been used to help determine the physical conditions of people. One researcher has discovered that the cries of a newborn baby can be analyzed and the analysis used to recognize certain health problems. An English zoologist, W. H. Thorpe, used sound spectrograms to study the calls of forty terns—birds that nest along the shores of the ocean. He found that adults uttered distinctive "fish calls" when they carried food to their young. The voiceprint of each tern showed clear individual variations of frequency, intensity, and duration, explaining why only their own young responded to their fish calls.

Law-enforcement officers have employed comparisons of voiceprints in presenting cases against suspects even though some people think that you cannot identify a person positively by this means. One interesting use of voiceprints occurred as the result of the Israeli-Arab Six Day War of 1967. In justifying their need to attack, the Israelis presented a tape recording which they claimed was made of a conversation between President Nasser of Egypt and King Hussein of Jordan plotting against Israel. Voiceprints were made from the tape, and then compared with voiceprints from a known speech made by Nasser. Dr. Lawrence G. Kersa, formerly of the Bell Telephone Laboratories, who prepared and analyzed the voiceprints, identified them as having been made by the same person.

In recent years, the Bell Telephone Laboratories have produced speech-like sounds by using electronic circuits in machines called *speech synthesizers*. One of these, the "Pattern-Playback" machine, works like a speech spectrograph in reverse: it produces speech from a spectrogram painted on a plastic belt. The machine scans the spectrogram with a light beam and translates the pattern into sound. Another kind of synthesizer uses a high-speed digital computer to produce speech from patterns punched on cards.

These machines were invented to help study the human voice, but they could lead to new devices, like a typewriter-operated voice. Using such a device, a person who was unable to speak could type his message and the machine would say it out loud for him.

Another possibility could be an automatic language translating system. This could combine a *speech recognizer* and a speech synthesizer. Two people who speak different languages could use this system to hold direct conversations, each speaking and hearing only his own language. Automatic devices would recognize speech in one language and translate it into the second language, synthesizing the sounds of that language.

A third possibility could be the talking computer that has become popular in science fiction. A computer could converse with the operator, listening to what the operator tells it (speech recognizer) and producing orally (speech synthesizer) the results of the analysis of the information fed it. The computer could talk back to the operator.

Animal Sounds
5

The National Symphony Orchestra settled down for its outdoor concert in Washington, D.C. There was the usual rustling of music sheets and last-minute plucking and adjusting of strings to be sure the instruments were in tune. The conductor raised his baton, signaling the opening bars of Prokofiev's *Peter and the Wolf*. In turn, each instrument that is identified with a character in the story was introduced, and played its theme. A flute was the bird; a clarinet was the cat; and so on through the remainder of the cast—Peter, his grandfather, the duck, the wolf, and the hunters. The audience, following the unfolding of the story in the music, gradually became aware of an errant flute. It was not located in the orchestra, but somewhere off to one side. The tune this flute played was correct, but it played the bird theme at times when it was not indicated in the score. This misplaced and undisciplined flute proved to be a mockingbird, imitating perfectly the flute in the orchestra, which, in turn, was imitating a bird.

Joining a symphony orchestra is not the only accomplishment of mockingbirds. In the days when mailmen used to blow whistles to announce deliveries mockingbirds learned to imitate them. Occasionally a mockingbird would imitate the whistle even when no mailman was near. This was a great annoyance to people who were expecting important mail. Some mockingbirds cry like cats, some mimic frogs, and all can reproduce the songs of other birds. This ability can be very upsetting to bird watchers, who, on hearing the call of a rare species, focus their glasses on the bushes and trees, only to discover that the singer is a mockingbird. Anyone who is deceived by a mockingbird need not feel foolish since the human ear cannot detect the fraud; a sound spectrogram is needed to distinguish the imitation call from the real one.

The mockingbird has not learned to imitate human speech, but other birds can. In addition to the well-known parrot, crows and ravens can be trained to croak some words and phrases. The birds with the most precise diction are the hill-mynah birds. These birds are natives of India and were brought to Hawaii in 1865 to help keep down certain insect pests. Mynahs are closely related to the common starlings that have been known to imitate cats and dogs. Starlings are much despised in this country as nuisances, but mynahs are used in psychology laboratories and are favorites as pets. People often try to get rid of starlings, but on the mainland of the United States, they pay high prices for mynahs. At least with birds, one might conclude that talk is not cheap.

One bird that unintentionally imitates a human sound is the basis of many folktales and superstitions. It is the limpkin, whose name comes from its curious limping walk, and it is found only in the swamps of Georgia and Florida. The Indians called it the crying bird, for it wails in the night with a sound like the forlorn cry of a lost child. People living along the borders of the Okefenokee Swamp or near Wakulla Springs, Florida, chill their listeners with ghost stories about the lost boys, fated to wander forever through the swamps, calling for help that never comes.

Songbirds, like humans, depend on their lungs for the energy to put sound waves in motion. A bird's voicebox is the *syrinx* that is located at the lower end of the windpipe (trachea) where it forms two branches (bronchi) which lead into each lung. This is a very different mechanism from the larynx, which is at the upper end of the human windpipe. The syrinx differs from one species to another. These differences determine whether the bird will hoot, whistle, croak, or sing a rippling song. The variations in the syrinx also affect a bird's ability to reproduce human sounds.

The syrinx contains a projecting membrane that vibrates in the stream of air from the lungs. The pitch of a bird's song depends on the tension of this projecting membrane

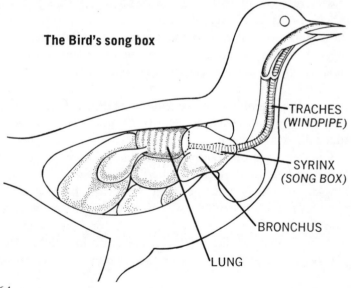

The Bird's song box

TRACHES (WINDPIPE)

SYRINX (SONG BOX)

BRONCHUS

LUNG

which is controlled by muscles. Listen carefully to a song-bird and notice the frequent change in pitch that makes up his song. On a recording of the voice of one song sparrow, there were 13 distinct song patterns and 187 minor variations. Imagine the precise control his muscles must exert on the membrane of the syrinx!

Other portions of a bird's vocal tract also influence its voice. The whooping crane has a five-foot windpipe that is coiled like a French horn. Its call, which humans describe as "ker-loo ker-lee-oo," can be heard by would-be-intruders over a radius of more than a mile. This is important for a bird that stakes out a 400-acre territory which he defends from other males of his species.

The whooping crane has a body size to match its majestic voice. It stands about five feet tall, and has a wingspread of seven feet. Its cruising speed when in flight is about forty-five miles per hour. Only about fifty whooping cranes survive today, but efforts are being made to protect them, both at their Texas wintering grounds in the Aransas National Wildlife Refuge on the Gulf of Mexico and 2,500 miles north, at their mating grounds near Great Slave Lake in Canada.

Birds use their voices for communication even though they have not developed what we would consider a language. Some birds that migrate in flocks use signals to assemble, to start flying, and to stop. Both male and female birds give warning calls. Young birds too can produce some call notes even though the syrinx of the young does not seem to be fully developed. Young birds respond quickly to the different call notes by which their parents warn them to crouch, remain motionless, or scatter when danger approaches.

Before the exodus from the nest, ducklings learn to recognize the mother duck's call. Within each species, there are slight differences among maternal calls. These are not discernible to the human ear, but you can spot them in spectrograms, and young ducklings can recognize the differences easily. There are also slight geographical differences in bird calls which can be compared to differences in human dialects. From species to species, however, the difference is greater, and can be distinguished by the human ear. For example, the maternal wood duck sounds like "kuk," while the mallard sounds more like "hut."

There seem to be some call notes which are recognized by most species of birds. These include the food calls of the young and the distress calls. There are many recorded instances of a parent of one species answering the insistent hunger call of the young of another species.

The distress calls of birds can be imitated to some extent by wetting the back of the hand, pressing the mouth against it as if for a kiss, and then drawing in air. With practice, a light kissing motion against the wet skin can produce a distress squeak. Some experts have been able to attract a number of birds of different species by hiding in the bushes and producing an imitation distress call.

The distress cackling of geese is considered by some people as a more reliable warning of danger than the barking of dogs, since geese have keener ears and sharper eyes than dogs. Geese once saved Ancient Rome from invasion by the Gauls by cackling loud enough to rouse the sleeping soldiers. Until recently, geese were used as sentinels on British outposts in Malaya. At present, a gaggle of fifty geese help guard a huge whiskey warehouse in Scotland to keep intruders from sampling the wares.

Among the songbirds, the male birds are the skilled songsters. In some species, only the adult males can produce songs, although both males and females use call notes. Young males usually cannot sing the mating calls or songs until they reach maturity the spring after they hatch. The male birds apparently use songs both to establish territorial rights and to attract females. Therefore, the long songs and mating calls are most commonly heard during the nest-building and mating season.

The mating calls of woodpeckers are not produced by the syrinx. Woodpeckers use their beaks to beat out a sharp, rapping tattoo, like the long roll of a drum, on a hollow limb or trunk of an old tree, or occasionally on the wooden shingles of a house. Woodpeckers' heads, from that of the large, nineteen-inch pileated woodpecker to that of the small, seven-inch downy woodpecker are specially formed to permit incessant drilling and drumming without damage to the brain. The bones of the skull are very thick and almost as hard as concrete. With this strong backing, a bird can chop away at a tree or telephone pole, or beat out a drum roll that can be heard in distant fields.

The ruffed grouse has an unusual method of producing his mating call. On moonlit nights, he stands in an exact spot on a fallen hollow log and beats his wings rapidly toward the log. The wings skim the log, but never touch it. Each fanning motion toward the log compresses the air between the log and wing, and each motion away from the log decompresses the air. The extremely rapid fanning motion creates sound waves that are intensified by the hollow log. The resulting whirring sound announces his presence, especially to any female grouse in the area.

Other birds, such as the Wilson snipe and the broadtailed

hummingbird, use the fast beating of their wings in the air as they swoop down to create their mating calls. The hummingbird can beat its wings as often as 200 times per second as it drives at speeds up to 64 miles an hour.

Insects too use sound for communication, including recognizing others of the same species. The story of the field crickets illustrates how their calls can be used to distinguish related species. For many years, *entomologists,* scientists who study insect life, believed that there was only one species of field cricket in the Western Hemisphere, but the field crickets knew better. Although the scientists were unable to observe significant body differences among the crickets they captured, the crickets recognized their own species by the songs of the males. A number of species may live side by side, but mating will occur only within a species—among those crickets whose male members sing identical songs. The repertoire of a field cricket includes seven different songs. By studying spectrographs of these calls, at least six different species were identified in the eastern United States. Experiments have shown that crickets that are hatched and raised in complete isolation from other crickets still produce the calls of their own species at maturity.

These calls include frequencies in the ultrasonic as well as in the audio range, as a group of mechanical-cricket inventors found out. They made a mechanical device that produced what they heard as a male cricket call. When they tried the noisemaker in the field, it failed to impress a single live cricket. The audio frequencies may have been perfect, but the absence of the ultrasonic frequencies was a giveaway as far as the crickets were concerned. Perhaps the crickets heard the call as you would hear a piano solo if the artist forgot to play any of the notes above middle C.

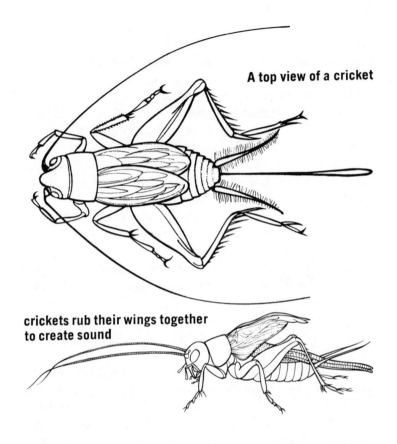

A top view of a cricket

crickets rub their wings together to create sound

Cricket calls are produced by *stridulation*—rubbing together of two roughened surfaces. Crickets, and also katydids and grasshoppers, have scrapers and files on the bases of their wings. When these are rubbed together, the entire wing vibrates, producing a chirping sound. Some people regard the chirps as a nuisance, while others find them a pleasant addition to the summer nights—to some it is noise, to others it is music. In several Oriental countries, it is the custom for people to construct cricket cages, and keep the caged insects in their houses. Not only do these people enjoy the cricket's songs, but they believe that a cricket in the house brings good luck.

Not all insect sounds that are produced by stridulation are as loud as the sound of the cricket. Some beetles produce quiet, squeaking sounds that are barely audible to the human ear even at a distance of two feet. These animals rub parts of their bodies together, but do not set their wings vibrating.

Perhaps the noisiest of the stridulating insects are the cicadas, including the species commonly called the seventeen-year locust. These insects have thin plates which cover deep pits in the abdomen. Membranes within the pits are set in motion by muscles attached to them, and this stridulation creates the sound.

In 1962, ant "talk" was first recorded. Ants make sounds by snapping their leg joints, scraping their feet, and rapping their jaws together.

About the same time, scientists discovered that honeybees "talk" as well as "dance" to communicate with each other. Ten distinctly different sounds have been identified in the hive. One type of sound occurs during the "dance" that some scientists believe informs the bees where a source

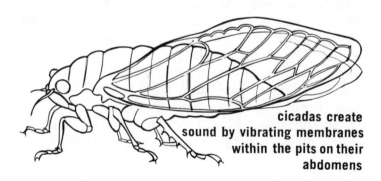

cicadas create
sound by vibrating membranes
within the pits on their
abdomens

of nectar is located. The variation in the length of this sound probably indicates the distance to the food site from the hive. Other sounds are characteristic of a young queen bee announcing her presence in the hive. Still other sounds are made by the workers while ventilating the hive. Of course, there are danger signals, and after the danger has passed, there is a "piping" sound which serves to soothe the hive. All these sounds are made by the rapid vibrations of the wings, ranging from 250 cps to 2,500 cps.

Flies and mosquitoes also produce sound by the rapid vibrations of their wings. Such sounds are used by insects to identify other members of the same species, especially at mating time. Man has taken advantage of the mosquito's mating call in an effort to reduce the population of these pests without destroying other wildlife or contaminating the earth.

The male mosquito is attracted by the buzzing sounds made by the wings of the female as she flies about trying to find a mate. The sounds are in the range between 300 cps and 800 cps. The male mosquito can hear only sounds that are less than 1 foot away, but he is attracted by any sound in the 300 to 800 cps range, whether the sound is produced by a female mosquito or by a mechanical device. If the sound is close enough, the male mosquito not only will fly directly to the source, but will clasp it with his claspers. So it is easy to set up a vibrating trap for male mosquitoes and destroy them before they mate. The only drawback is to be able to place enough traps close to enough male mosquitoes.

A less successful recent attempt to take advantage of insect calls was *Project Bedbug,* intended for use in jungle warfare. Scientists have found out that bedbugs produce excited sounds when approached by a warm, walking, human meal. The idea was to hang containers of bedbugs along hidden jungle trails near camps so that the approach of an enemy patrol would be signaled by the sounds from the hungry bedbugs. The sound, of course, would be amplified electronically (see page 114), since these insects do not normally make noises loud enough to alert their walking or their sleeping prey. The project was not too enthusiastically accepted by soldiers in the field. Perhaps they did not wish to add imported bedbugs to the many pests that already made their lives in the jungle miserable.

If the sound of bedbugs is unwelcome in the jungle, there is a sound in the marshes and swamps of the eastern part of the United States which is greeted by nearly everyone. It is the call of the male spring peepers. The persistent peeping that spreads across the land is a more certain sign of spring than a whole flock of robins. After the silent nights of winter, suddenly the twilight hours are alive with the shrill call of these thumbnail-size treefrogs. The spring peeper depends on the vocal cords of his larynx for his mating call, as does his larger cousin the leopard frog and his giant cousin the bullfrog.

The bullfrog, which measures from eight to ten inches in length, is the largest of the North American frogs and it is the noisiest. The deep-throated call of the male bullfrog is created by air being driven back and forth between his mouth and lungs while his lips and nostrils are closed. The sound is amplified by the swelling of the floor of the mouth, creating a large pouch or sound chamber. The female is comparatively silent, for she is only capable of producing the piercing scream that both sexes emit when captured by a hungry enemy such as a snapping turtle.

Oddly enough, the world's largest frog cannot croak. The *Conraua goliath* of Africa's equatorial west coast grows over two feet in length, may weigh more than seven pounds, and can leap ten feet in one jump. Yet this frog, with a head as big as a saucer, cannot call his mate because he lacks vocal cords.

Generally, people are most familiar with the sounds made by animals setting their vocal cords vibrating. They recognize the dog's bark, the cat's meow, the mouse's squeak, the bear's growl, the cow's moo, the sheep's baa, and the lion's roar. But vocalization is not the only means of animal communication. Remember the woodpecker, the hummingbird, and the snipe. Another example is the beaver who warns his fellows of danger by slapping the surface of the water with his tail.

For centuries, men thought that the waters of the rivers, lakes, and seas were silent except for the occasional slap of a beaver's tail or the splash of a fish surfacing. Most people doubted that fish, which have no larynx, were able to make any other sound, although they knew that fish could hear. During World War II, ships were equipped with instruments to detect the sounds of enemy submarines (see page 115). The sailors soon found themselves hearing things that definitely were not submarines. The "silent" ocean was giving forth with clicks and squeals, grunts and whistles, rattles and bangs that never originated in the engine of a submarine. The sailors were eavesdropping on the previously secret sound-world of fish and other sea animals.

Since the war, scientists have spent a considerable amount of time exploring this newly discovered sound-world. Hydrophones are lowered into schools of fish to find out what sounds they make while they swim together. The whistles of dolphins and the beeps and squeals of whales have been recorded. The scientists discovered that sound serves water animals in much the same way that it serves land animals. Sound is used for communication: to attract mates, to warn of danger, and, in some cases, to establish territorial rights. Perhaps because vision is more limited under water, sound plays a greater role for sea animals in interpreting the environment than it does for most land animals. Light, even in clear waters, becomes so dim at a depth of 100 feet that it is impossible to distinguish colors; at 1,000 feet, there is not sufficient light to discern the shapes of nearby objects; and below 1,700 feet, the ocean is pitch black. Since they cannot see much, marine animals that spend all or part of their lives in the ocean deeps often have very efficient sound systems.

Some sea shrimp have special noise-making claws which they snap vigorously. Some fish gnash their teeth and scrape their fins against their scales to produce sounds by means of stridulation. Such fishes as the damsel fish, sea trout, and toadfish have special muscles that vibrate their *swim bladders* to produce sounds like drum rolls. The toadfish creates a "boop" that resembles a foghorn and can be heard out of the water. Underwater, at a distance of two feet, the sound of the toadfish can reach an intensity of over 100 decibels, about as loud as a pneumatic drill. The swim bladder is a gas-filled cavity within a fish's body that is used primarily to change the density or weight of the fish so that it matches the density of the surrounding water and allows the fish to maintain its position at various depths. Beside producing sound and acting as a stabilizer, in some species of fish the swim bladder also plays an important role in the hearing process.

Sea mammals probably produce the most complex communication sounds of all sea animals. When a killer whale was caught in a net in the Pacific Ocean off the coast of British Columbia, his distress calls attracted an entire pod of whales. Killer whale sounds have been extensively taped and analyzed. Their "voice" range is from about 50 (cycles per second) to over 40,000 cps (40 kHz)—a far greater range than the most talented opera singer. And because water is a better conductor of sound than air, the distance the whale's "voice" travels is also impressive. Hydrophones have picked up killer whale signals at a distance of three miles and it is believed that the whales can hear the sound at even more distant points. The variety of sounds the killer whale can produce is evident from such descriptions as: "bleats," "blares," "squeals," "cries," "wails like a lovesick cat," and "clicks like a hundred carpenters hammering nails into a roof."

In 1970, Dr. Roger S. Payne of Rockefeller University spent several weeks recording the sounds of the humpbacked whale in the waters off Bermuda. He found that the whale's song was strangely beautiful. It had a definite melodious pattern and repeated theme which lasted from five to thirty minutes and included elements that sounded like high-pitched groans and yelps, with occasional gigantic sneezes.

The musical quality of the tapes Dr. Payne made, using underwater microphones, attracted the attention of many musicians. Pete Seeger, the folk singer, based his composition, "The Song of the World's Last Whale," on them. Another folk singer, Judy Collins, used the tapes as a background for her arrangement of "Fairwell to Tarwaithie," a song about whalers. And Alan Hovhaness, the symphonic composer, wrote an orchestral work that included some of the actual taped melodies. His piece, "And God Created Great Whales," has been played by such leading orchestras as the New York Philharmonic and the Philadelphia.

A whale has no vocal cords; it produces sound in its larynx. The sound is emitted through the blowhole when the animal surfaces to breathe. When the whale submerges, a strong muscular flap seals the blowhole shut, keeping out both sound and water. But this does not stop the whale from communicating. Underwater, the sound waves are transmitted from the larynx through the whale's flesh to the surrounding water. And, if all this isn't enough, the whale can produce a considerable amount of sound by setting the water vibrating (*hydrodynamic disturbances*) when he thumps and splashes with his tail flukes and also when he heaves his big body completely out of the water.

While only a few killer whales live in captivity, several species of their close relatives, dolphins and porpoises, are commonly kept. Although there are differences between porpoises and dolphins (porpoises have spade-shaped teeth while dolphins have cone-shaped teeth, and porpoises are generally smaller than dolphins), many people use the names interchangeably. Both are really small whales. Actually, the killer whale is a kind of dolphin, and the friendly dolphin and porpoise kept in captivity have the same sharp teeth as the killer whale.

Since it is easier to work with and study individual animals in a confined place than to work with an entire pod of whales swimming free, most studies of the sea mammals' ability to communicate use porpoises rather than killer whales. Furthermore, porpoises are smaller and less expensive to feed. Not only are they friendly to man but they are

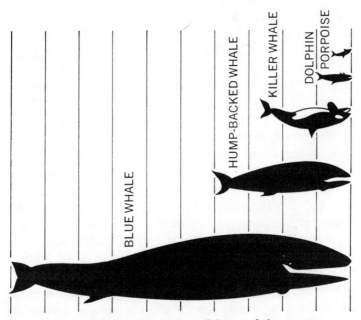

BLUE WHALE

HUMP-BACKED WHALE

KILLER WHALE

DOLPHIN

PORPOISE

cooperative in playing his games. Many of these games are carefully devised by scientists to test the sea mammal's intelligence and his marvelous vocal tract and hearing ability. Recently, porpoises have been taught to help men by fetching and carrying tools for underwater work. The animal does this in response to sound signals from a pinger, an underwater signaling device.

If dolphins cannot really talk to each other, they come closer to that human accomplishment than any other animal. Studies of the dolphin's whistles, only one of the many kinds of sounds the animal makes, have shown that different whistle patterns have different meanings. Dolphin mothers and their children, if separated, repeat one whistle pattern continuously until they are reunited. The distress-call whistle of the dolphin will bring others rushing to its aid, and if the distressed individual is badly injured, the rescuers will work together to lift it out of the water so that it can breathe. A mother dolphin about to give birth uses a special whistle pattern that brings another female dolphin to her side. This animal stays with the mother until the baby is born, and then helps her take it to the surface for its first breath of air.

Analyses of the whistle patterns show that at least eighteen separate whistle sounds are used. These whistles are further analyzed to determine the frequency with which they occur and their positions in a whistle pattern. This technique is similar to the method used to break secret codes or to translate a long-dead language written in strange symbols. The results seem to show that the dolphins have at least an elementary whistle language. Whistle languages are also used by some humans. The vineyard workers of Gomera, one of the Canary Islands, use a whistling language, and whistling sounds are parts of Mixtec, Zapotec, Otoni, and other Indian languages spoken in central Mexico.

As men gathered knowledge about the dolphin, they became intrigued by the idea that someday they could learn to talk with dolphins. Two possibilities have been explored. One is to break the "dolphin code" so that men can "talk dolphin" as they would another foreign language. The problem with this approach, at least in part, is that the dolphin has a frequency range that possibly goes as high as 200,000 cps (200 kHz), far beyond the human ability to create or even hear sound. It is quite possible that, if dolphins really have a language, a good part of it is produced in frequencies above the human voice range. This difficulty might be solved by using mechanical devices to produce the high frequencies. Such a method might permit men to communicate with dolphins, but it would not be as simple as sitting down for a quiet chat with a friend.

Another approach to man-dolphin communication is to teach the dolphin to speak a human language. A few dolphins have been taught several words and phrases. One dolphin learned to say "All right, let's go!" at the beginning of training sessions. Other dolphins have learned to say a few words in a high-pitched, Donald Duck-like voice. When their voices are taped and then played back at a slower speed, the words are more intelligible. But so far, there has been nothing to show that the dolphin is doing more than imitating its human friends. Certainly, the day when man and dolphin can communicate directly through language is still in the future.

Efforts are also being made to teach a limited English vocabulary to chimpanzees. After two years of training, one of these animals could say "mama," "papa," "cup," and "up." It is interesting that in order to teach the chimpanzee, it was necessary to hold its lips in the proper positions so that the sounds from its larynx would be formed into words. After a great number of such assisted practice sessions, the chimpanzee was able to say the words by itself. Considering the hours of patient training that were required to teach these four words, it is unlikely that men and chimpanzees soon will be communicating freely through human language.

In the meantime, chimpanzees in the wild seem to do very well in communicating with each other. They use simple sounds, such as low grunts of appreciation when they are eating desirable food and spine-chilling "wraah's" when they are angry. And throughout the world, various kinds of monkeys use many "word" signals. Recently, scientists have found that the vervets of Africa use a special "snake chatter" to warn other monkeys of the presence of a cobra or puff adder in the jungle. They use a two-unit phrase followed by a seven-unit phrase; they also use a single bark to announce a threat from an eagle or a cheetah. Their language includes "lost baby cries" and the "wow!" and "woof, woof" of the mature male. As time goes on, scientists will undoubtedly discover more and more animal sounds. They will find out how they are made and what they mean.

TRANSMITTING SOUND

The Speed of Sound

6

A blind man sat erect in his chair facing a white screen. A round velvet target, suspended from the ceiling, hung in front of the upper left-hand corner of the screen. The man made clicking sounds with his tongue. Sounds like "tische tische" could be heard as he slowly turned his head from side to side. First one ear and then the other faced the screen. The blind man changed the clicks to a hiss. It sounded as if he started to say "six," but got stuck on the "s." He nodded his head as if he had come to an agreement with himself, and told the observer that the target was velvet, and he described its location perfectly.

The velvet target was removed, and a metal disk was hung in a different position in front of the screen. The blind man repeated his sounds and head movements. Once again, he correctly identified the target's material and location. The tests continued. Without sight or touch, he recognized the material, even distinguishing between metal and wood and between velvet and denim. He could tell whether the target was small or large, and he knew when it was moved even a few inches.

Magic? No. This blind man was only using a well-developed form of something which is often called the "sixth sense" of the blind. The five senses of man are sight, hear-ing, touch, smell, and taste, but many blind people seem to have a sixth sense. Yet, even a blind person finds it difficult to explain what it is that causes him to stop short of an ob-stacle in his path. In ancient times, this strange ability was considered miraculous, and blind people were sought out by those who wished to know what would happen in the fu-ture. If a blind person could predict an obstacle in the path ahead, surely the gods had given him a "second sight" with which to predict what lay ahead in time, as well.

Scientists were unwilling to accept the sixth sense as an explanation of this ability of blind people. They looked for a more rational answer—an extension of one of the usual five senses. But which one? At first, it was thought that a blind person could feel a very slight change in air pressure when he approached an obstacle. The scientists reasoned that movement forward pushed the air forward, but an ob-stacle, such as a wall, stopped the forward movement of the air. Thus, the pressure of the air between the forward-mov-ing person and the wall was changed. The change was so slight that most people would not feel the difference. A blind person, however, undistracted by sight, would feel the pressure change, and would respond automatically. The sci-entists believed that the face was most affected by such changes in pressure. Instead of a sixth sense, they spoke of "facial vision," and considered it an extension of the sense of feeling.

Once a theory is proposed, scientists try to prove it. At Cornell University, Dr. Dillenback began a series of experi-ments in 1940 to test the facial vision of a group of blind people. He placed a screen at a distance ahead in the path of the blind people, and found that they became aware of the presence of the screen well in advance if they were wearing shoes and were walking on a bare floor. When barefoot, they came much closer before they discovered it. And when they walked barefoot on a thick rug, they almost walked into the screen before they realized it was there. Obviously, since the change in air pressure was the same in each case, facial vision could not explain the results. However, they can be explained by two well-known facts about sound.

First, sound can be *reflected*. It can be bounced back by certain surfaces as a ball is bounced back from a wall. The reflected sound is called an *echo*. The clicking and hissing sounds of the blind man in the first experiment were reflected from the various targets. In the second experiment, the sounds of the blind people's footsteps were reflected from the screen.

Second, sound travels at measurable speeds or *velocities*. You do not hear a sound at the instant it is made. There is an interval of time between the making of a sound and the hearing of that sound. The interval may be so brief that you do not notice it, or it may be long enough for you to time it with the second hand of a watch. The length of the interval depends on the speed of the sound and on the distance between you and the source of the sound. The blind man in the first experiment was far enough away to hear echoes and judge the positions of the targets by the differences in the length of time before the echo returned to him. The scientists who were studying the sixth sense of the blind began to call it *echolocation*—an extension of the sense of hearing.

YOU CAN EASILY PROVE that sound does not travel instantaneously. The next time you hear a jet plane flying above, look in the direction from which the sound is coming. Even in the clearest sky, you will not see the plane where you think it should be. However, if you look ahead, you will see the plane. The sound is coming from behind because you hear the sound the plane made when it was in a previous position.

Imagine for a moment that you are standing in a place where you have a clear view for miles in all directions. A jet plane is about to fly in a straight line over your head. You will be able to see the plane before you can hear it coming, and you will still hear its noise after it vanishes from view. Actually, the plane is no longer precisely where you see it either. But the speed of light is very great. The distance the plane travels while the light from the plane is reaching you is so small that you see the plane in almost its original position.

During World War II, the people of Europe were frequently reminded of the difference between the speed of sound and the speed of light. Bombs could be seen falling before the eeerie whistling sound that accompanied their fall could be heard.

Every thunderstorm is proof that light moves faster than sound. Unless the lightning strikes very close indeed, you see the flash before you hear the thunder, since light travels through air about one million times faster than sound. It takes sound about 1 second to travel $\frac{1}{5}$ mile through air, so YOU CAN ESTIMATE the distance to the point where the lightning struck. If the interval between the time you see the flash and the time you hear the sound is 5 seconds (count slowly to five), the lightning occurred 1 mile away. If the interval is 20 seconds, the distance is 4 miles. To find the distance, divide the number of seconds by 5.

YOU CAN SET UP an interesting demonstration of the

Gassendi, for whom a crater on the near side of the moon was named. They used the new second-measuring pendulum to time the lag between the flash and the explosion at a measured distance from a cannon. Their rather crude experiment showed the speed of sound to be about 1,400 feet per second.

Other scientists later improved Mersenne and Gassendi's method and got more precise results. Instead of one cannon, two were used—one on each of two hilltops. The distance between the two cannons was measured. One dark night, when the flash could be clearly seen, one of the cannons was fired. Observers on the other hilltop measured the interval between when they saw the flash and when they heard the shot. Next, the observers turned cannoneers and fired their cannon. Back at the other hill, the interval between the cannon's flash and its roar was measured.

Two cannons were used because the scientists were concerned that the direction and the speed of the wind would change the interval of time it took the cannon's roar to travel from one hilltop to the other. Anything that is likely to change, and so affect the results of an experiment is called a *variable*. In this experiment, the scientists hoped to eliminate the wind as a variable by measuring the time interval in opposite directions—against the wind and with the wind. If they repeated the test several times, they would have enough observations to figure an average speed. In some experiments, the scientists eliminated the wind entirely by using the Paris sewers. They measured the length of time it took a sound to travel from one end of a sewer to the other.

Wind is only one variable that affects the speed of sound. When sound is traveling through air, the temperature is an

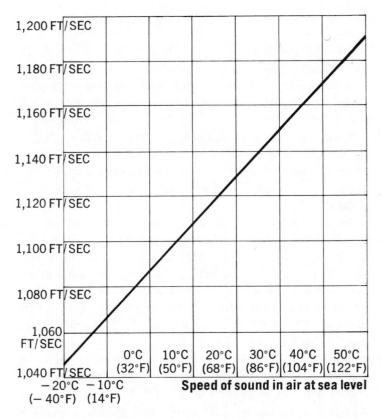

1,200 FT/SEC							
1,180 FT/SEC							
1,160 FT/SEC							
1,140 FT/SEC							
1,120 FT/SEC							
1,100 FT/SEC							
1,080 FT/SEC							
1,060 FT/SEC	0°C	10°C	20°C	30°C	40°C	50°C
1,040 FT/SEC	(32°F)	(50°F)	(68°F)	(86°F)	(104°F)	(122°F)

−20°C −10°C   **Speed of sound in air at sea level**
(−40°F) (14°F)

important variable. On a clear, windless night, with the air
temperature at 0° C (32° F), the sound of the cannon travels 1,088 feet per second. If the temperature of the air is
20° C (68° F), the sound travels 1,129 feet per second. On
a very cold night, with the temperature at −20° C (40°
below zero F), the sound travels only about 1,047 feet in a
second.

A change in the temperature of the air affects the *density*
of the air—the amount of air (mass) in a given space (unit
volume). As the temperature of the air rises, the air ex-

87

pands. As the temperature decréases, the air contracts. YOU CAN PROVE this for yourself. Blow up a balloon until it is firm but only slightly inflated. Tie its mouth closed tightly. Measure the distance around the balloon with a tape measure or piece of string. Place the balloon in a warm place, such as in bright sunlight. After another hour, measure the balloon again. It will be larger. (If the balloon is inflated too much—if the rubber is stretched too much—the balloon may burst when you put it in a warm place.)

Inside the balloon, the amount of air does not change, but the density of the air changes. As the temperature rises, the same amount of air expands to occupy a greater amount of space. The molecules of air are spread out more, and so the air is less dense. The less dense a given material is, the faster is the speed of sound passing through the material. The more dense a given material, the slower the speed of sound in it.

The *elasticity* of air also affects the speed of sound. If you think of elasticity only as the property that permits a rubber band to snap back after it has been stretched, you may find it strange to think of air as elastic. But elasticity means more than that. Elasticity is the property that causes a substance to return to its original shape and size after it has been changed or deformed by any stress or strain. For example, suppose you had a piece of sponge rubber. If you pound it with a hammer, the pressure from the hammer will compress the rubber and deform its shape by putting a dent in it. When you remove the pressure, the sponge rubber will return to its original shape and size. If you pull on the rubber, it will be stretched, and its shape will be deformed. Stop pulling, and the rubber returns to its previous shape and form. If you hold both ends of the sponge rubber and twist it, the shape will be changed, but the rubber will resume its original shape when you let go of the ends. You can combine the deforming forces by crumpling the sponge rubber into a ball or by pulling as you twist. In each case, when you remove the force, the rubber returns to its original shape and form.

If you were to treat a piece of Styrofoam in the same way, the results would be very different. Styrofoam is a lightweight material, usually white, that often is used to make picnic chests, ice buckets, disposable cups, artificial snowballs for Christmas trees, and many kinds of store-window decorations. If Styrofoam is pounded, twisted, or pulled, it will crush or break; it never returns to its original shape and size. Foam rubber is very elastic; Styrofoam has little elasticity.

Both foam rubber and Styrofoam are solids. They have definite shapes and sizes (volumes). But air, as a gas, has neither a definite shape nor volume—unless it is confined in a container. To test the elasticity of air, it is necessary to confine it in a container. Suppose you have an airtight box that can unfold like an accordion. If you pull out one side of the box, the air inside will move to fit the new shape of the box. If you push the side of the box back, the air will resume its original shape and size. If you push the side of the box further in, the air will be squeezed together in the box; both its shape and size will be altered. When you release the pressure on the box, the air in the box will push back on the side of the box. If the side could move freely (if there were no friction), the air would push the side until the box returned to its original size and form. The air, too, would regain its original volume.

You can readily understand the importance of the elasticity of the air if you look back at the diagrams of sound waves on page 23. As each succeeding pulse moves through the air, the air is in turn squeezed (compressed) and allowed to expand (rarefied). If air were not elastic, the first crest that reached it would squeeze up the air like a pounded piece of Styrofoam. The crests that followed would pile up behind; they would be unable to move on.

The speed with which sound travels through air is of tremendous importance in these days of fast jet airplanes. For many years, scientists and engineers assumed that the speed of sound was the limit beyond which no plane could fly. In fact, they believed that no plane could survive reaching the speed of sound because as an object approaches the speed of sound, the air exerts an ever-increasing drag on that object. This drag is caused by the limit of the elasticity of the air. The molecules of air in front of the plane cannot move out of the way fast enough.

The disturbance in the air created by the jet engine sends out waves above, below, to the sides of, behind, and ahead of the position of the engine at the instant the energy is released. The sound waves above, below, at the sides, and behind the plane form a trail or a wake somewhat like the disturbance a boat propeller creates in water.

If the plane is moving slower than the speed of sound, the plane will never catch up with the energy in the sound wave ahead of the plane. If the plane is moving faster than the speed of sound, the sound wave can never catch up with the plane. The nearer a plane reaches the speed of sound in the air around it, the greater the drag. This came to be known as the *sound* or *sonic barrier*. It was believed that no plane could be built with enough power to break

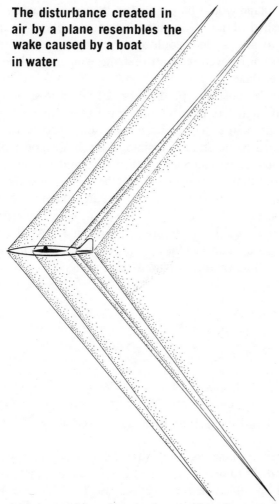

The disturbance created in air by a plane resembles the wake caused by a boat in water

through the sound barrier. And even if a plane could break the barrier, some people thought that the heat generated by the drag would affect the plane. Furthermore, they believed that the plane would be trapped in the sound wave, and as both rushed along at the same speed, the plane would be shaken to pieces, and would drop from the sky. Even the most optimistic were certain that the wings would be torn from the plane.

But these most dire predictions did not stop some scientists and engineers from aiming for a plane that would fly faster than sound. There are always some people who are determined to do the impossible. They built model planes of various shapes and tested them in wind tunnels. They discovered that by sweeping back the wings, in what came to be known as the delta-wing shape, and making the wings as thin as possible, the drag on the plane could be reduced, although it could not be entirely prevented. At the same time, heat-resistant metals were developed for use in planes, and more powerful jet engines were designed.

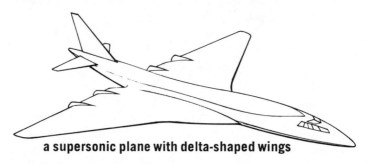

a supersonic plane with delta-shaped wings

Finally, a plane was built that theoretically had the necessary power to break the sound barrier. But the entire project was shrouded in mystery because the U.S. Air Force considered the test a military secret. Although the flight took place on October 14, 1947, the public did not even hear rumors about it until the end of December, and the

Air Force did not admit the event or release any details until the following June. How could such a secret be kept? It was simple: the flight took place at Muroc Air Force Base in the middle of the California desert. There was no one for miles around the huge base, and no reporters were allowed on the base.

The plane, a Bell XS-1, was small, only 31 feet long and 11 feet high with a wing span of 28 feet. The empty plane weighed only 4,892 pounds, but it carried 8,000 pounds of fuel. Because the plane's cabin was very small, a slim, short man was selected as pilot. Captain Charles E. Yeager may have been small in stature, but he was big in courage. He had been a fighter pilot in World War II, and he had been shot down over France. With the help of the French underground, he escaped on foot to Spain, and eventually reached England. Even though he was entitled not to fly in the war zone again, Captain Yeager insisted on returning to active duty.

With his usual bravery, Captain Yeager began his now famous supersonic flight. No one knew what would happen. Some were certain that the plane and pilot soon would be little pieces plummeting back to earth. But most believed that the plane would break the barrier, and Captain Yeager would fly faster than sound and return safely to earth.

The XS-1 was carried under the belly of a huge bomber, and Captain Yeager rode with the crew. The bomber took off and climbed steadily. When it reached an altitude of 30,000 feet, Captain Yeager climbed through a hatch and into the cabin of his tiny plane. The XS-1 was released from the bomber, and Captain Yeager fired its four rocket engines. The plane thrust forward, reaching a speed of 1,000 miles per hour, and the few observers in that lonely desert area below heard the first *sonic boom*. The test was a success. The problem of creating a plane that could fly faster than sound had been solved, but man had created a new problem for himself—the sonic boom. (See chapter 10.)

The term *Mach 1* is now used to indicate the speed of a plane that is flying as fast as sound under certain conditions. It was named for Ernst Mach, an Austrian physicist who studied the flow of air. Twice the speed of sound is Mach 2. Captain Yeager's plane attained a speed of about Mach 1½ since the speed of sound at the altitude at which he was flying is 662 miles per hour. Apollo XI, returning the first men from the moon, entered the earth's atmosphere traveling at a speed of about Mach 32. When it slowed down enough to break through the sound barrier, it created two sonic booms—the second was the echo reflected from the surface of the ocean.

Reflecting, Absorbing, and Directing Sound

== 7 ==

The first time a young child stands in a tunnel or cave or at an "Echo Point" or "Echo Lookout" and calls "hello," he is apt to listen with awe to the returning echo. Like primitive men, who in the past may have stood and called in the same place, he may believe that there is someone answering from the other side. Maybe there are men over there somewhere, hidden from sight. Or perhaps the replies come from spirits, friendly or unfriendly, who dwell in the rocks and trees. There is a feeling of magic about echoes that can never quite be erased even when you understand their scientific explanation.

Echoes are everywhere around you. Walk along a quiet street at night, and your ears will pick up the sound of footsteps that seem to originate somewhere behind you. If you walk faster, the speed of the following footsteps increases. If you slow down, so do the mysterious footsteps. A quick glance over your shoulder shows that there is no one in sight. You stop; the footsteps stop. You start walking; the footsteps begin again.

The phantom footsteps are only the echoes of your own footsteps. Just as you can bounce a ball off a wall and catch it with your hands, so sound can bounce back and be caught by your ears. The sound created by your feet slapping against the sidewalk bounces off the walls of the buildings along the street. You hear the sound behind you because you and your ears have already passed beyond the place where your feet made the sounds and where the sounds are being reflected from the walls.

When you create an echo by calling across a valley, your voice is reflected by rocks on the far side. In this case, the sound is directed in front of you, and your words are repeated from positions in front of you.

If you know the speed of the sound, YOU CAN USE a stopwatch to determine roughly the distance between you and the wall of rock across the valley that reflects your voice. Start the watch as you call out "hello." When the echo returns, stop the watch. Suppose the watch shows that it took the sound of your voice 10 seconds to cross the valley and return as an echo. This means that it took 5 seconds to reach the rock on the other side and 5 seconds to return. Therefore, the distance to the rock must be 5 times the distance the sound travels in 1 second. If it is a calm day and the temperature is 20° C (68° F), the speed of the sound is 1,129 feet per second. The distance between you and the rock is 5 times 1,129 feet or 5,645 feet—a little more than a mile.

Of course, the above result is just an approximation. If you could run a tape measure from your mouth to the surface of the rock, it is highly improbable that the distance would turn out to be exactly 5,645 feet. The lack of accuracy is due in part to the fact that you can only approximate the speed of the sound; remember that for each degree Centigrade increase in the temperature of the air, the speed of sound increases about two feet per second. Furthermore, you have physical limitations that make it almost impossible to obtain an accurate measurement in this way. First, there is the question of whether you really pushed the button to start the stopwatch exactly when the sound left your mouth. Second, it is almost certain that you did not push the button to stop the watch exactly when the sound reached your ears. The energy that caused the sound had to travel from your ears to your brain, and then the impulse needed for pressing the button had to be sent from your brain to your finger.

Even a tiny fraction of a second has meaning when you are working with speeds like 1,129 feet per second. An error of even $\frac{1}{100}$ of a second in timing would mean a difference in distance of more than 11 feet. For this reason, this method cannot be used to measure, or even approximate, the locations of nearby echo walls from which the echoes return in a second or less. But there are devices that can make such measurements automatically for many purposes.

Echoes that follow the original sound too closely cannot be heard as echoes. The distance at which this occurs varies slightly depending on air temperature (which affects the speed of the sound) and on individual hearing ability. Generally, a distance of more than 25 feet is necessary to hear an echo. This is because the human ear needs a time interval of about $\frac{1}{20}$ of a second to hear sounds separately. If the time between the sounds is shorter, the ear hears them as one continuous sound.

The next time you are in a long, quiet hall with an uncarpeted floor and a smooth wall at one end, TRY THIS. Walk toward the smooth wall at the end of the hall. The echoes of your footsteps will sound louder as you approach the wall, and they will also be heard closer and closer to the original sounds of your footsteps on the bare floor. As you come near the wall, the echoes seem to stop. You can hear no echoes reflected from the wall, but the echoes are still there. You stop hearing them because your ears can no longer distinguish the echoes as separate sounds; they are occurring too close to the original sounds. If you walk toward the wall several times, listening carefully, you will be able to determine the distance from the wall at which you can no longer hear echoes.

Not all living things share man's limitations in echo detection. Some bats are far superior to men when it comes to hearing and interpreting echoes. Bats have always been associated with witches, wizards, and other creatures of superstition because their uncanny abilities to move swiftly and safely through the dark were thought to be due to supernatural and evil powers. Even today, no Halloween party is considered complete without bat decorations. But a bat's remarkable ability to fly unerringly around all obstacles in the darkest night is proof not that the bat is in league with the devil, but rather that it has a sensitivity to echoes that far exceeds that of a man using a stopwatch. A bat does not call out "hello" in its dark cave, but the bat does emit sound waves. It uses the echoes of these waves reflected from the walls of the cave and from obstacles in its path to guide its flight.

In 1793, Lazzaro Spallanzani, a professor at the University of Pavia in northern Italy, discovered an amazing fact about bats. If he covered their eyes, they could still fly about easily and catch insects. But if he covered their ears, they bumped into objects much as people bump into things when they are blindfolded. This information, while interesting, was hardly helpful at that time since the bats were not making sounds that man could hear. Almost 150 years passed before scientists could explain Spallanzani's discovery.

Although most people were aware that some people could hear better than others, few suspected that sound beyond the hearing of any man was a possibility. Not until 1883 did scientists first begin to write about ultrasound, and the invention of the silent dog whistle was probably the first time such sounds were used by man. The dog whistle emits sounds with frequencies too high for the human ear to hear (as high as 20,000 cps—20 kHz), but well within the hearing range of dogs since they can hear frequencies up to 50 kHz. The "miraculous" dog whistle first appeared on the market in the late 1890s.

In 1920, an English scientist, H. Hartridge, suggested that bats could steer in the dark by means of sound waves beyond the range of human ears. His theory could not be proven at the time because scientists did not have instruments for detecting such sounds.

The ultrasonic cries of bats were not detected until 1938 when Dr. Donald R. Griffin and Dr. G. W. Pierce invented a new kind of microphone that could pick up sounds in the ultrasonic range. These sounds were then changed to electrical impulses that could be observed as lines on an *oscilloscope*—a machine that shows on a screen changes in electric current. The bright dots of light moving across the green fluorescent screen enabled the scientists to discover that the little brown bat, which lives in caves and deserted buildings in most parts of the United States, could send forth cries in the range between 40 kHz and 80 kHz. This tiny bat, smaller than the common house mouse, can produce as many as 60 of these ultrasonic cries in one second. Recent researchers found that not all bat sounds are ultrasonic. Some sheath-tailed bats produce frequencies as low as 12 kHz that are audible to man.

little brown bat hanging upside down in a cave

Once there was proof of the bat's ability to emit ultrasonic sounds, the next step was to show that the bat used these sounds in avoiding obstacles in the dark. Several bats were released in a room in which fine wires had been strung

in every direction. Although the wires were not more than
$3/16$ of an inch in diameter, the bats flew safely about the
room, never once bumping into the man-made maze. However, if either a bat's mouth or a bat's ears were covered,
that bat bumped into the wires as clumsily as a man would
in an unlit room. The echoes of its high-pitched screams
warned the bat whenever an obstacle lay ahead. This phenomenal steering mechanism of the bat is known as echolocation. (See page 83.) Echolocation is not useful in detecting objects smaller than the wavelengths of the sound a bat
emits. For example, spider web strands are not readily detected, and some tiny bats can be entangled in them.

Most bats use echolocation in their unending search for
food. Some bats that eat fruit and the nectar of flowers use
their senses of sight and smell to find their food. A few
kinds of bats eat fish, and some suck the blood of animals.
But most of the 2,000 different kinds of bats eat insects,
and the echoes reflected from the bodies of insects serve
them very well. Small bats, like the little brown bat, consume half their weight in insects each night. A little brown
bat can consume 150 large insects or 5,000 very small insects per hour. Mexican free-tailed bats that live in Texas
eat at least 6,600 tons of insects per year. With so many insects to catch, a bat's ultrasonic voice must be kept very
busy.

Unlike the wires strung across the room, however, the
bat's intended prey do not always stand still or even fly
along in a straight course awaiting the bat's swoop. Moths,
which are a favorite food of some bats, have been found to
have hearing in a range from about 3 kHz to 150 kHz.
Thus, the moth can hear the bat's high-pitched shrieks, and,
like an airplane in a dogfight with another plane, the moth

can twist and turn in an effort to escape the enemy. In addition, some moths use another trick to defeat the bat. Tiger moths respond to ultrasonic waves by making audible clicks and ultrasonic noises of their own. The latter interfere with the bat's echoes and confuse the bat so that it does not have a clear target. And so, the intended meal frequently can escape.

Whether the bat is flying toward a moth, a wire, or the rock wall of its cave, its ultrasonic sounds are echoed back toward it. How does the bat know which objects are in its path? How can the bat decide whether to attack, dodge, or land? The cries that it sends out are the same. The differences must be in the returning echoes. Obviously, contact with an object must affect, must in some way change the sound.

The next time YOU CALL OUT from some echo point or in a tunnel, listen to the returning echo. Does it sound exactly like your voice? Or, has it been changed somewhat by being reflected from a rock wall?

When you call across a valley, there may be only one echo. But if you stand in the center of a cave and shout "hello," the sound reverberates all around you, and you hear many echoes as the sound bounces back and forth off the walls. This happens because sound moves outward in every direction from the point at which it is created. The sound you make strikes the walls of the cave all around you, and each time it strikes, an echo is created. These echoes, in turn, strike other parts of the cave wall, creating new echoes.

A sound wave moving outward through air uses up the energy that created it as it presses the molecules of air before it. The farther a sound wave travels, the more energy is spent. Since the loudness of a sound depends on the energy remaining when it reaches the hearer, as a sound wave travels onward, its loudness decreases. It finally becomes only a soft murmur, and then is heard no more. And in the cave, the echoes finally die out when all the energy that caused the original sound is used up.

The walls of a cave are excellent for creating echoes because most, or all, of the sound is reflected from them. But not all solid obstacles affect sound in the same way. Some materials absorb all, or most, of the sound. Most materials fall in between these two extremes; they reflect some of the sound and absorb some of it.

Man is always seeking to change and control his environment, and sound is a very important part of the human environment. Depending on his needs or desires, man may wish to increase a sound, decrease a sound, or suppress it completely. One way to do this is to change the surfaces from which the sound is reflected or by which it is absorbed.

There is nothing new about the idea of manipulating the sound environment, but now people are doing it to cut down on sound pollution. No one worried very much about the dangers of sound pollution until recently. In the past, the plaster walls and ceilings of buildings were thick, the exterior walls were brick, stone, or wood, and it was not uncommon to have a brick filling between the outside walls and the interior walls, making a total thickness of at least a foot. In luxury buildings, like the famous Dakota apartment house in New York City, the walls are even thicker. The Dakota was built in 1880, and has walls that are three feet thick. The walls of modern apartment houses may be no more than nine inches.

103

YOU MAY WISH TO COMPARE these thicknesses with the walls in your home. Open a window, and use a ruler or yardstick to measure the distance from the face of the exterior wall to the face of the interior wall. How many inches of sound-absorbing and sound-reflecting material lie between the inside of your house and the outside noises?

The problem is not only that we are building houses with less massive construction. We are also living closer together, and we are making a great deal more noise both inside and outside our homes. In the fourteen years between 1955 and 1969, the noise level in the United States doubled. Now, the noise level in the United States is growing by 1 decibel each year. Quiet country roads have been replaced by limited-access highways and turnpikes where trucks and cars roar along day and night. Nearly every homeowner with a patch of grass around his house has a noisy power mower, and many people have snow blowers to clear their driveways during the winter months. Howling jet airplanes crisscross the sky with increasing frequency, and almost every river, lake, and oceanfront is plagued with snarling motorboat traffic.

Inside the house, the increase in the sound level is also bad. The din of washing machines, clothes dryers, dishwashers, vacuum cleaners, food blenders, and mixers is accompanied, in many cases, by the noise of water banging through the plumbing. Popular music seems to be most appreciated when its decibel rating is highest, so the radios, record players, and TVs are tuned all the way up and blare forth. In cities, the ears of apartment dwellers may receive not only their own household sounds, but those of an increasing number of neighbors. We seem to be living in an era of "hear thy neighbor." High-rise apartment buildings, even when surrounded by grassy land, concentrate large numbers of people on comparatively few square feet of ground. A single high-rise apartment tower can house more than 1,500 people.

The noise level has reached the point where scientists regard it as a serious menace to health. Not only can sound pollution cause loss of hearing, but many believe that it is a factor in a long list of illnesses, among them stomach ulcers and heart trouble, and may even harm unborn babies. Yet, it would be hard to find anyone willing to go back to the good old days of hand-washed clothes and dishes, travel on horseback and in rowboats, and a silent stereopticon for entertainment. Few people would trade their power machines for the comparative quiet of a hand mower and a snow shovel. However, the problem can be approached in other ways: by making man's mechanical aids operate more quietly (see page 149), and by placing sound-insulating barriers between the sources of the sounds and the human ears.

It is possible to construct almost totally soundproof rooms called anechoic chambers. (See pages 7–8.) The Bell Telephone Laboratories in Murray Hill, New Jersey, and a few other research centers have such rooms. The Bell Telephone "dead room" is a noise stopper in two ways: it prevents sounds from entering from the outside, and it stops all sound waves dead when they reach its walls, thus making it echo-proof.

The dead room is 38 feet wide, 38 feet long, and 45 feet high. All six surfaces—walls, ceiling, and floor—are covered with 5-foot wedges of fiberglass. Since fiberglass wedge floors are definitely not intended to be walked on, a net, made of strong steel wires, is strung across the room to support the workers and their equipment.

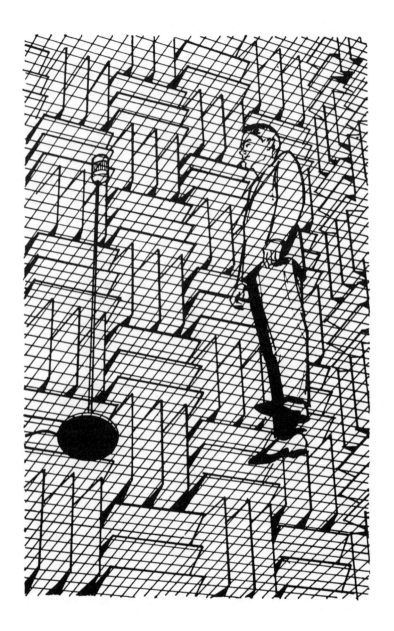

Since smooth surfaces are such good reflectors of sound, the wedge-shaped blocks were used to create a jagged effect. The blocks were made of fiberglass because it is a very porous material, and is readily penetrated by air. The energy of sound waves entering this material is absorbed in its maze-like inner structure. The thicker the fiberglass, the more it can absorb. The 5-foot wedges of the dead room are capable of absorbing almost all sound.

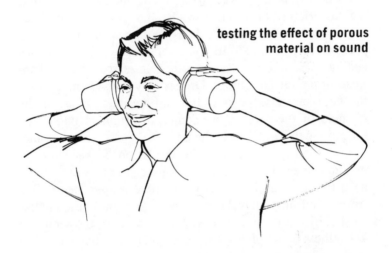

testing the effect of porous material on sound

YOU CAN TEST the effect of a porous material on sound by using several Styrofoam cups. Hold a cup tightly against each of your ears. To what extent do the cups muffle the sounds around you? Now try using stacks of two or more cups over each ear. Do you notice a difference in the intensity of the sound when you use more than one cup over each ear? Does the Styrofoam absorb more of the high-pitched or low-pitched sounds?

Five-foot walls of fiberglass or Styrofoam would not be practical for the average home, either in terms of cost, or in the amount of space needed. Fortunately, we do not need, and in fact, would not live in, truly soundproof rooms. Soundproofing for normal purposes means reducing noise to an acceptable level rather than eliminating all noise. However, methods similar to the construction of the dead room can be used in modern buildings. The spaces between the walls can be filled with fiberglass or other sound-insulating materials. For exterior walls, this not only provides soundproofing but also insulates against summer heat and prevents loss of heat to the outdoors during winter. Porous ceiling tiles, often called *acoustical tiles,* can be used instead of plaster on ceilings. Drapes on windows and rugs on the floors are also porous, and can be added to make the surfaces of the room more sound absorbing. Upholstered furniture can be placed in the room to soak up more sound.

Few modern homes provide insulation between rooms, but apartment builders are becoming more aware of the need for such insulation, at least between apartments. One story about the thin walls in a new apartment house in New York City points up the need. Two people were listening to a Beethoven symphony that they had just tuned in on a radio. They could not agree what movement they were hearing. One said, "It's the second." His friend said, "Oh, no! It's the third." And a voice from the apartment on the other side of the wall added, "You're both wrong. It's the fourth." This incident will not be repeated in the houses built in New York City in the future because the new building code sets standards for sound transmission between apartments—no more than 35 db.

New York is the first American city with such a code,

but the United States generally has been very slow in recognizing the importance of soundproofing in the construction of homes. Many European countries already have regulations that set standards for required sound insulation in multiple dwellings. There are standards for airborne sounds, such as traffic noises, and also for sounds that pass through floors and ceilings, such as the sound of footsteps overhead. The Federal Housing Administration has prepared a list of recommendations for soundproofing in the United States, but these are voluntary. Some apartment building owners, tired of complaints about noisy neighbors, write into their leases a requirement that at least a certain percentage of the floor space in the apartments must be covered by rugs. Rugs serve not only to reduce the noise in the apartment but also to protect the tenants in the apartment below. Such precautions are not necessary in the old Dakota. There, the floors were built with double concrete insulation beneath surfaces of solid oak.

Occasionally soundproofing is carried too far. When *Time,* Inc. built its $70 million office building in New York City, the soundproofing was so efficient that it cut out the normal street noises. With this background of noise gone, typewriters seemed unnaturally loud, and voices carried so well that private conversations were almost impossible. The workers missed the familiar noises, and were quite unhappy. Fortunately, the solution was not too difficult. The architects were able to increase the noise of the building's ventilating system, and the building was a success.

Acoustics has concerned architects from earliest times. In theaters, for instance, sound must carry to all parts. Probably the earliest examples of good acoustics in theaters resulted from accident and not from any definite understanding of sound; thus, the theories may have resulted from practice.

Marcus Vitruvius Pollio, whose work in Rome spanned the period between the later part of the first century B.C. and the beginning of the first century A.D., evidently gave considerable thought to the science of sound. Vitruvius, as he is usually called, was architect for the Emperor Augustus. His ten-volume work, *De Architectura,* has been translated into English, and is still in use. It contains directions for providing good acoustics in the outdoor amphitheaters that were so much a part of ancient Roman life.

Vitruvius mistakenly thought that the voice was "a flowing breath of air," but he did recognize that sound moves outward in every direction and that it is important that there be no obstacles between the source of the sound and the ears of the hearers. For this reason, he advised builders to follow the example of even more ancient builders and always place the seats in ascending rows so that the people in front would not block the sound from those behind. This arrangement also allows everyone to have a clear view of the stage. Vitruvius' work was much used in the construction of buildings in Europe during the Renaissance, and even modern theater builders follow the seating plan that he recommended so many centuries ago.

One would suppose that with all our present knowledge of sound, modern architects could plan theaters and music halls with assurance that they would be nearly perfect. Strangely enough, this is not always so. Each major music hall that is constructed is an individual case, and the outcome seems to be no more predictable than the temperaments of the prima donnas who will perform in it. Excellent examples are Alice Tully Hall and Philharmonic Hall,

both in Lincoln Center in New York City; one was a gem, the other was a dud.

For many years, the New York Philharmonic Orchestra, which is acknowledged to be one of the great orchestras of the world, performed in Carnegie Hall. Carnegie Hall had exceptionally good acoustics, but it was getting old and shabby. When the decision was made to build Lincoln Center as a home for the performing arts in New York, it was almost inevitable that the Philharmonic would be moved. Many people protested the move, and predicted that no new hall could ever compare with the beloved Carnegie. Music lovers picketed those who would tear down the old hall, and eventually raised enough funds to save and refurbish it.

But in the meantime, plans for the new hall were underway. Use was made of all the latest developments in the field of acoustics; outstanding acoustical architects planned even the most minute details. Finally, on September 23, 1962, Philharmonic Hall was opened with great ceremony. The event was a big social success, but as one reporter described it, the hall was "an acoustical catastrophe." Seven years and 2 million dollars later, a series of extensive changes produced a good but not perfect hall.

The acoustics are still far better when the orchestra practices in the empty hall than when a concert is being given. On the one hand, the bodies of the audience soak up some of the sounds, especially the bass notes. On the other hand, the presence of an audience causes some unwanted sounds which are highly magnified. For example, during the opening concert of 1969 in the redesigned hall, the conductor stopped the performance of the first selection to shake his musician's finger at photographers in the observation booth; the clicks of their cameras were too loud and were interfering with the sounds of the orchestra. It is only fair to point out that the conductor, Seji Ozawa, has a very sensitive and well-trained ear.

At one point in their search for better acoustics, the architects used acoustical clouds on the ceiling of Philharmonic Hall. In the past, acoustical vases have been used. Vases for the improvement of acoustics were described by Vitruvius, but none was discovered until 1961. Then four such vases were found by archeologists, digging in the ruins of the amphitheater at Nora, an ancient city on the southern coast of the Mediterranean island of Sardinia. The vases were made of terracotta, a red-brown, hard-baked pottery, and were five feet tall and three feet eight inches in circumference at the widest point. Both ends of the vases were open and slightly tapered. The vases had been placed in a low wall that formed the front of the stage. There, they served to amplify the voices of the actors and to direct them over the heads of the orchestra, which was seated in front of the stage.

An actor can scream loudly enough to be heard in the last row of the top balcony of a theater. However, whispered words of love or conspiracy have difficulty reaching the same place. Singers and actors train their voices so that they can be heard clearly, but still some mechanical aid is helpful. Even the ancient Greek actors used such devices. The Greeks were very fond of the theater, and many of today's plays and movies come directly or indirectly from authors who thrilled Greek audiences so long ago.

Since Greek theaters were outdoors, making sure that the actors' voices were heard in the last row was a big problem. One way Greek actors increased the power of the human voice was to speak through masks with funnel- or trumpet-shaped mouths. The trumpet masks concentrated the energy of the voice in one direction, forward—rather than allowing it to spread out in all directions. The trumpet masks made the voices sound strange, but the concentration of energy meant that people in front of the trumpet could hear more clearly even though they were not close to the actor. The masks were very ornate, and each actor was proud of his collection. Modern theaters are often decorated with copies of Greek masks that represent tragic and comic characters. The principle of the trumpet used in the masks was used again 5,000 years later when Thomas Edison invented the phonograph; he put a trumpet on the early models to direct the sound toward the listeners.

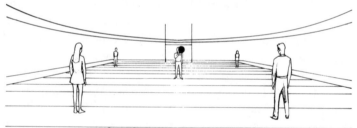

testing the effect of a megaphone

YOU CAN FIND OUT how well the trumpet shape works by using a megaphone, which also directs sound. If you cannot borrow a megaphone, make a large cone from stiff cardboard. You will need four or more friends to help you, and you will have to try your experiment in an open field. Ask your friends to take positions in front, in back, and to the left and right of you. Speak in a normal voice as your friends slowly walk away from you. Each should stop when he can no longer hear your voice. He can then mark his position with a stone or stick. When all the positions are marked, repeat the experiment, but this time, speak through the megaphone. Is there any change in the hearing distance for any of your friends? Who can hear you for the shortest distance, and who can hear you for the longest distance?

A modern form of the megaphone that has become very popular is the bullhorn. In this, the human voice is amplified electronically before it is directed out through the trumpet. Bullhorns are often used by outdoor speakers so that their voices can be heard over the street noises.

Electronic amplification through microphones and loud speakers is also used in many theaters today to bring the voices of the actors and singers to the audience. Microphones may be concealed behind footlights or even in the sets on the stage. But more often, they are skillfully concealed on the actor or singer himself. In the old days, most opera stars were, if not fat, at least very substantially built. People thought this was necessary in order for the singer to have a powerful enough voice to be heard throughout the opera house. The result was that, in some cases, the heroine, who was supposed to be wasting away from ill health or unrequited love, had the figure of a professional wrestler. Whether or not the modern, small, easily concealed microphone, slipped down the neck of her dress, deserves the credit, it is very noticeable that slender opera stars are singing these roles today.

Sound in Water and in Solids

8

The submarine moved swiftly through the water. Inside, a young sailor listened intently to the sounds from the instrument in front of him. The knocks and groans did not worry him. He knew that they were produced by a sperm whale that had wandered in close to the underwater banks. Nor was he bothered by the sizzling sound that reminded him of fat dripping onto the hot coals of a barbecue fire. He recognized it as the sound of the snapping shrimp that are common in the middle latitudes—between 45° N and 45° S— where the water is no more than 30 fathoms deep. The sailor-technician was concentrating on the whistling sounds: porpoises and blackfish make whistling sounds, but sometimes the hydroplanes or rudders of a submarine can produce the same sound. Aboard a warship or a submarine, the sonar technician cannot afford to mistake one for the other.

The technician was using a *passive sonar* instrument— one which only receives sound but does not emit any sounds of its own. He was listening to the sounds of the undersea world. Just as the air around us seems, at times, to be filled with sounds, so the ocean is alive with noise. Water possesses the necessary qualification for transmitting sound: it is elastic. YOU CAN TEST how well water carries sound the next time you go swimming or even the next time you take a bath. Put one or both ears underwater and give the surface of the water a sharp slap. You may be surprised to find that water carries sound better than air does.

To make it easy to remember, we usually say that sound travels four times as fast in water as it does in air. You can appreciate why that is only a rough figure if you remember that the speed of sound depends on temperature and density. (See page 87.) In seawater, the speed of sound depends on the pressure and salinity (saltiness) of the water as well as on its temperature. The range of temperature change in the ocean is very great. For example, a submarine cruising near the surface of the ocean in the tropics may be surrounded by 85° F water. If the submarine dives 450 feet, the change in water temperature can be as much as 30° F. Furthermore, a sister submarine, slipping along near the surface in polar regions, moves through water that is near the freezing point. The rate of change of the speed of sound is from 4 to 8 feet per second for each 1° F change in water temperature. Thus, if the pressure and salinity are the same, sound can travel more than 400 feet per second faster toward the submarine cruising in 85° F water than toward its sister ship in the Arctic Ocean.

Sounds travels faster in water that is under pressure. In the depths of the oceans where as much as 36,000 feet of water may be piled up, the weight of the water above exerts tremendous pressure on the water below. The average change in the speed of sound in water due to pressure is 2 feet per second for each 100 feet of depth. Since sound travels more rapidly when the pressure on the water is increased, you would expect it to travel faster in deep water than in water near the surface, but this is rarely the case. The increase in speed is canceled by a decrease due to the other factors: temperature and salt content.

The saltiness of the oceans is by no means the same throughout the world. Fresh water weighs about 62.4 pounds per cubic foot. The average weight of seawater is 64 pounds. The difference of over 1½ pounds represents the weight of the salt in a cubic foot of seawater. The amount of salt in the water is figured in parts per thousand, usually written as ‰. The average amount of salt in ocean water is about 35 ‰. Near the mouths of large rivers, or where great quantities of ice are melting, the salt content may be very low. Salinity in the Baltic Sea is between 2 ‰ and 7 ‰. In other areas, there may be more than 30 times as much salt present. The "hot, salty holes" of the Red Sea have as much as 257 ‰. Sound travels 4 feet per second faster for each ‰ of salt in the water. This could mean a difference of more than 1,000 feet per second between the speed of sound near the mouth of a large river and the speed in water with a high concentration of salt.

The variations in the speed of sound in water are of great importance to the sonar technician on a submarine who is listening for enemy subs and ships. He must allow for these variations when he reports the location of the origin of the sound he detects. We can picture the effect of these variations if we imagine that the source of a sound is inside a perfectly round, balloon-like, rubber sphere. As the sound moves outward, the sphere expands and expands.

In the air, at ground level, sound moves outward in all directions at a steady pace. If no object is in its way, the

difference between the speeds of light and sound if you can use a football field or some other large open place. Ask someone to stand at one end of the field and pound slowly but at regular intervals on a drum or on the bottom of a large pan. The drummer should use a stick that is large and bright enough to be seen from a distance. (A stick covered with aluminum foil works very well.) If you stand at the other end of the field, you will notice that the drummer will just be raising his stick instead of striking the drum each time you hear the beat. The effect will be like that of a movie when the sound is not synchronized properly and the actor's voice follows slightly behind the movements of his lips.

Almost anyone can observe that the speed of sound is not instantaneous, and so it was inevitable that men would attempt to measure it. But before such measurements could be made, two things were needed: a way to measure small intervals of time, and a way to create a loud sound and a bright light simultaneously. The introduction of gunpowder into the western world in the thirteenth century made the latter possible. You can see the flare from a distant cannon before you can hear the explosion. However, it was not until the 1640s that a satisfactory timepiece was made. The famous Italian scientist Galileo had studied pendulums, and knew they could be used to measure time. But he died in 1642 before he could make a pendulum whose swing would occupy a convenient fraction of a minute (then, the smallest standard interval of time). Two years later, his French student Marin Mersenne made a pendulum just the right length to measure $\frac{1}{60}$ of a minute—one second. In 1685 Christian Huygens, the Dutch astronomer, made the first pendulum clock using Mersenne's pendulum.

Mersenne worked with another French scientist, Pierre

shape of the imaginary balloon is not changed; only its size is increased. If we imagine a dot on the outside of the balloon, that dot will move outward in a straight line. This will happen because, near ground level, there will be very little change in the temperature and density of the air. The sound wave that reaches the ear, like the dot on the sphere, will have traveled in a straight line.

Imagine now that the rubber sphere is expanding outward through the waters of the ocean. Where the water is warmer, that part of the sphere expands more rapidly. Where the water is colder, that part moves more slowly. Water pressure and salt content will also change the speed at which parts of the original sphere move. Soon the balloon

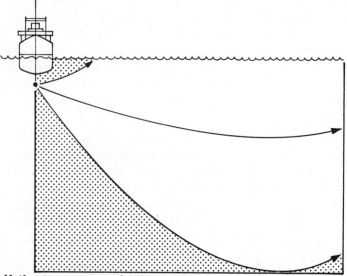

if the temperature is the same, the speed of sound increases with depth (greater pressure) and the sound is bent upward

will no longer be a sphere. Some parts will be farther from the source of the sound than other parts. The dot on the surface of the rubber probably will not have moved outward in a straight line from the source of the sound; the sound wave will have been bent.

In the ocean, increased pressure and increased salinity bend the sound upward, while decreased temperature bends the sound downward. In general, the sound sent down into the ocean from a ship is bent upward by the pressure and downward by the colder temperatures at the lower depths. This results in the sound following a gradual downward curve from the source through the water.

In a few places, such as the Red Sea, the water is warmer

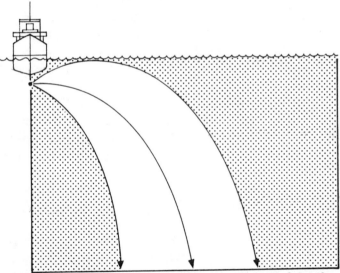

however, the effect of temperature greatly outweighs the effect of pressure. Therefore, the speed of sound decreases with depth (lower temperature) and the sound is bent downward

below the surface than it is near the surface. At a depth of 1 mile in some parts of the Red Sea, the temperature may be over 100° F. As a result, both temperature and pressure bend the sound waves upward in a sharp curve.

All these changes in speed are of even greater importance when the sonar technician aboard a submarine or ship is operating *active sonar*. With active sonar, the operator does not wait for the object to reveal its presence by making sound. Instead, the operator directs sound waves outward and uses the returning echoes to locate and identify the objects.

The active sonar transmitter has an electrically powered *oscillator* that produces strong electrical pulses. These are sent to a *transducer*—a device that converts energy from one form to another. The transducer uses the electrical energy to produce high-frequency sound waves, which it sends out through the ocean waters. In the transducer, electrical energy is changed into kinetic energy (motion). The energy received from the oscillator then becomes the motion that creates the sound waves in the water.

Sound itself, unlike heat, light, motion, and electricity, is not usually considered a form of energy. Sound is the result of motion (kinetic energy). It is the motion of the particles in the material through which the wave moves that creates sound. However, you may at times read about "sound energy." The writer may be assuming that you understand this as a form of shorthand for the energy actually involved in the transmission of sound.

The transducer of the active sonar also receives energy from the returning echoes and changes it into electrical energy. Since much of the energy sent out by the transducer is lost during passage through the water, the returning echo is much weaker than the original impulse. So, the electrical signal that results from the returning echo is made stronger by an amplifier. The amplified signal is then changed back into sound, and the sonar operator can hear the returning echo through headphones or a loudspeaker.

Modern sonar also provides for sending some of the amplified signal through a cathode-ray tube. Then the signal is flashed on a screen similar to a radar screen. This makes it possible for the operator to see the shape of the object and its location in relation to his own position.

When active sonar was first developed, it worked somewhat like a searchlight. Sound waves were sent out in only one direction at a time. This meant that at any moment, the ship was blind in all but one direction. Modern sonar sends out waves in a 360° sweep—a full circle—so that the ship can search in all directions at the same time.

Sonar beams use high-frequency waves that fall within the range of audible sound. The frequency used is determined by the limitations of the human operator. The human ear is most sensitive to sound waves in the range of from 1,000 Hz to 2,000 Hz, but it does not take much imagination to guess what would happen to an operator who had to listen to a high-pitched squeal for hours. Therefore, a more pleasant-sounding 800 Hz frequency, about the same as G_5 on the piano, is used.

At first, active sonar was used only on surface vessels and passive sonar only on submarines. Today, not only are ships and submarines equipped with both, but airplanes also can take advantage of sonar. *Sonobouys* can be dropped from an airplane into the sea. These instruments detect underwater sounds and echoes. They are equipped with radio transmitters that relay what they detect by means of radio waves to the airplane.

Although modern sonar was developed to meet military

121

needs, it has also been put to work in scientific research. In the past, when scientists wanted a sample of the ocean floor, they would drill a hole and bring up a core. They could drop a drill down through several miles of water to reach bottom, but they could drill only a short distance into the ocean floor—only until the drill tip wore out. They could not replace the drill tip and reenter the same hole. Now, with the use of sonar, a new tip can be installed, and the drill can be replaced in the hole to continue digging into the ocean floor.

The sonar systems for these drills are made up of two parts: sonar beacons on the rim of a funnel which remains in the drill hole on the ocean floor, and a sonar homing device on the drill. After a new tip has been attached, the drill is lowered, and the homing device monitors the signals sent out by the beacons on the funnel in the hole. The homing device operates water jets in the tip of the drill which nudge the drill from side to side until it is properly centered over the funnel and can reenter the hole.

Another nonmilitary use of sonar is the *fathometer* found on most commercial ships and on many private pleasure boats. The fathometer is used to measure the depth of the water by sending sound waves down from the hull of the ship to the ocean bottom. Energy from the returning echoes is amplified and used to record a line on moving paper. The line represents the time it took for the sound wave to descend and the echo to ascend. This line is read in fathoms to determine the distance from the ship's hull to the bottom—the depth of the water beneath the ship. When a series of readings is recorded, the resulting graph is a profile of the ocean bottom.

The simplest use of the fathometer is as a navigational

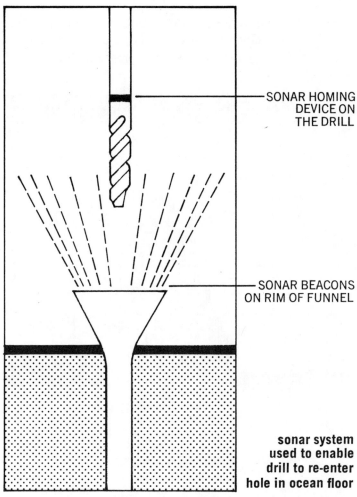

SONAR HOMING
DEVICE ON
THE DRILL

SONAR BEACONS
ON RIM OF FUNNEL

**sonar system
used to enable
drill to re-enter
hole in ocean floor**

instrument. It is used to keep a ship in a safe channel when
the ship might run aground on a sand bar, coral reef, or
other unseen underwater obstacle. Sound waves can travel
freely through even the murkiest water where light waves

could not penetrate for even one foot. This makes the fathometer especially valuable in rivers such as the Mississippi, which every day carries more than a million tons of

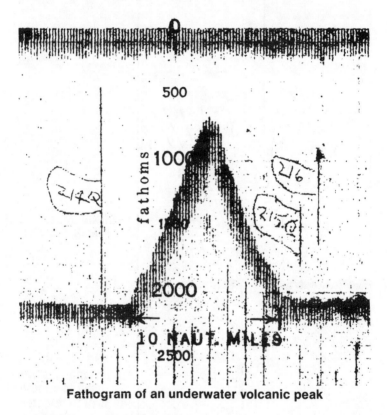

Fathogram of an underwater volcanic peak

sediment to the sea. The river sometimes deposits part of its silt in boat-trapping loads along the way. At other times, it may gradually fill old channels while it is scouring out new channels elsewhere on the river bottom.

The fathometer is one of the most useful instruments of the United States Coast and Geodetic Survey, which prepares the charts that are necessary for all water navigation. The Coast and Geodetic Survey did a complete survey of Long Island Sound in 1888. At that time, the water depth was measured by hand. The surveyors used a weight at the end of a long line. The line was marked to show distances from the weight. A surveyor lowered the line until it touched bottom and recorded the distance according to the mark on the line at the surface of the water. Then the line was laboriously raised, only to be lowered again a little farther on.

In 1969, the Coast and Geodetic Survey ship "Whiting" resurveyed Long Island Sound. This time, measurements were made by a digital fathometer. Instead of a line profile like the one shown in the last illustration, this fathometer produces a series of numbers in very small print, etched in gray graphite on a chart. Each number represents the depth of the water at mean low tide for that particular position. For each position, the fathometer makes 40 to 50 readings to ensure accuracy. As many as 4,000 readings are taken for a square mile of the sea bottom being surveyed.

Interestingly enough, the bottom of Long Island Sound changed very little in the eighty-one years between the two surveys. Unfortunately, the same cannot be said for the waters of the Sound, which are badly polluted near the cities and villages that line its shores. Because of excessive pollution, there is reason to fear that, in far less than the next eighty-one years, the western end of the Sound may fill in and become a salt marsh.

How far can sound travel underwater? There is, of course, no one answer, for it depends on the volume and

125

the frequency of the sound wave and on the temperature, pressure, and salinity of the water. But we do know that it is possible to send sound waves through at least 12,000 miles of water. A 200-pound charge of TNT exploded off the southern coast of Australia was heard on hydrophones 2,600 feet beneath the waves off the coast of Bermuda. The sound had traveled a great-circle route around the Cape of Good Hope, finding its way around islands and shallow areas in its path, and arrived in the Bermuda waters 223 minutes later. This means the average speed of the sound was about 3,200 miles per hour or more than 4 times as fast as sound travels in air at sea level at 20° C.

Of course, it was no accident that the hydrophones in Bermuda picked up the sound waves of the distant blast. It was part of an experiment being conducted by the Lamont Geological Observatory of Columbia University. Dr. Maurice Ewing, Director of the observatory, had been investigating undersea sound channels since the early days of World War II. These *Sofar channels,* the name is an acronym for *SO*und *F*ixing *A*nd *R*anging, carry sound for great distances through the waters of the oceans.

Sofar channels are formed not by physical boundaries, such as pipes or even underwater mountain ranges, but rather by temperature and pressure boundaries. And, strange as it may seem, these channels are made up of the waters in which sound travels most slowly. To understand this, it is helpful to think of the ocean as divided into two layers. In the layer at the top, sound is bent downward because the temperature decreases as one moves downward from the surface. In the bottom layer, the temperature remains about the same. Therefore, sound is bent upward because the pressure of the water increases with the depth.

When an explosion is set off where the two layers join, the sound is sent out in every direction. However, the sound that moves upward is bent back because of the temperature factor. The sound that moves downward is bent up because of the pressure factor. The result is that a significant part of the energy that is transmitted by the sound wave ends up in the channel where the two layers join. This increased amount of energy is sufficient to carry the sound of the explosion through the ocean waters halfway around the earth.

Sound also travels through solid materials. If you have ever been in a building while a plumber was at work on the pipes in the basement, you are aware that metals carry sound very well. Furthermore, sound waves travel about fifteen times as fast in steel as they do in air. YOU CAN TEST the sound-conducting ability of metals by using a long metal table or an exposed pipe. Place a wristwatch on one end and rest your ear against the table or pipe at the other end. If you cannot hear the watch tick immediately, slowly move toward the watch, keeping your ear on the metal surface. From how much farther away can you hear the tick of a watch through metal than through air?

If you have two metal tables, place them so that the ends touch. Place the watch on one table, and rest your ear on the other. If you cannot hear the tick, move toward the watch, keeping your ear on the metal surface. Where must your ear be to hear the tick? What is the effect of a separation in the metal on its ability to carry sound waves?

Now use a wooden table or long board. Place the watch at one end so that the grain of the wood runs from your ear to the watch. At what distance can you hear the tick? Try listening to the watch across the grain of the wood. At what distance can you hear the tick?

If you ever looked closely at a piece of raw wood, you probably noticed that the harder and the softer parts of the grain alternate. The harder parts are denser than the softer parts. When sound moves across the grain of wood, it is bent each time it moves from one part of the grain to the next. This constant bending requires a lot of energy, and therefore, the sound cannot travel very far. In the case of the two metal tables together, no matter how you push them, some space always remains between them. The metals are not continuous. Again, energy is lost in crossing the gap.

The behavior of sound waves as shown by the two metal tables and the wooden table is the basis of a device, an ultrasonic scanner, that is very important to modern industry. Sound is used to examine the interior of metal objects such as the girders in bridges and high-rise buildings. For this type of work, ultrasonic frequencies are generally used. The device sends sound waves into the material and receives the returning echoes. Any hidden bubble, crack, or other defect will change the path of the reflected sound.

There is nothing new about the idea of inspecting the interior of metal objects for defects. The earliest approach, and one that is still in use in many factories, is to remove items at random from the production line, and then take them apart and examine the interiors with a microscope. If an entire batch is faulty, this method probably will discover the fault. If only one or two items are faulty, they may escape the sampling. Moreover, the method is slow, and all the items examined are destroyed—they cannot be used.

Another common method is X-raying. More items can be

examined by this method, and good items are not destroyed. But this method is expensive, and the results cannot be determined until each X-ray picture is developed. Furthermore, doctors are questioning the affect of excessive use of X-rays on the human body.

By far the best method now being used is ultrasound, which is quick, comparatively inexpensive, and safe. Ultrasound can complete in ten seconds an examination that requires ten minutes with the X-ray technique. Using an ultrasonic device, one factory that makes automobile axles is able to inspect its entire daily output of 18,000 axles, thus insuring that no defective product is sold.

In the manufacture of airplanes, it is essential that the metal used in the parts be free from defect. Ultrasonic inspection can be used to detect defective new metal, but after the metal is in use for some time, the constant vibrations to which it is subjected can cause defects. This *metal fatigue,* as it is called, can be fatal if it is not discovered in time. Strain gauges usually have been used in airplanes to help the mechanics discover tiny cracks. But now ultrasound can be used to show weaknesses in the metal even before the tiniest crack appears. Small transducers, built into the airplane frame in the areas most subject to strain, can send ultrasonic waves into the surrounding metal and receive the echoes. The transducers operate while the plane is in flight so that the pilot can be instantly aware of any developing weakness.

The success of sonar in exploring metal was not ignored by those scientists who were exploring the interior of the human body. X-rays had revolutionized the world of medicine both in the diagnosis and treatment of many illnesses. But X-rays can be dangerous, especially when they are used repeatedly. Ultrasonic sonar, as far as is known, has no effect on the human body, and it produces very accurate pictures when the energy carried by the echo is passed through a cathode-ray tube. Ultrasonic sonar has been particularly helpful in diagnosing brain damage.

Sonar has been put to some very peculiar uses as, for example, at Cornell University. Dr. James R. Stouffer gathered together a group of experts, staff and students from the animal science department. He asked them to examine two pigs and determine which would produce the leaner meat. Even after very thorough examinations, the group could not agree on which was the leaner pig. Dr. Stouffer then began his examination, using a curious-looking instrument of his own invention. He fitted a track over one animal's back, and started a transducer gliding rapidly along the track. The ultrasonic echoes were changed into electrical energy, which, in turn, was changed into light energy. The latter appeared as blips skipping across an oscilloscope. He repeated the process with the other pig. (The blips showed clearly which was the fatter pig.) An examination such as this can be very valuable in developing a breed which is less fat. In the past, the only way to be sure a pig was lean was to slaughter it, a procedure that made further breeding rather difficult.

As we have already found, the animal world did not wait for man to develop sonar before putting it to use. The bat and the whale have used ultrasonic waves since before man learned to write his history and maybe even before man appeared on this planet. These animals act as their own transducers, both sending and receiving sound waves, and they are much more efficient in their use of sonar than is man with his complex instruments. But man is trying to refine his instruments and produce personal sonar systems.

Now there are scientists who see in sonar "eyes for the blind." Most of these *ultrasonic guidance devices* look rather like small flashlights with wires leading to earplugs. The "flashlight" is the transducer, and the energy of the returning echoes is changed into electrical energy that travels through the wire to the earplug. In the earplug, the electrical energy is used to produce sound again.

As the wearer of the device approaches an obstacle, the pitch of the sound becomes lower, warning him that something is in his path. Using these devices, blind people have been able to thread their way through an obstacle course of barrels, boxes, and trees. Some of the devices can also produce changes in the volume of the sound that the wearer can interpret to determine whether the obstacle ahead is hard or soft.

One objection to the presently available sonar devices for the blind is that the earplugs shut out other sounds that the blind need in order to move about safely. So scientists are still trying to find ways to help the blind develop their own natural echolocation ability. No one pretends that man will ever match the dolphin or the little brown bat when it comes to echolocation, but experiments like the one on pages 97–98 show that man can learn to use and improve this formerly unsuspected talent.

Hearing Sounds
9

If a tree deep in the forest falls and no one hears it fall, was there any sound? This is a question that has been debated by philosophers for hundreds of years. But now, since science has discovered the existence of ultrasonic and infrasonic waves, perhaps the question should be changed to "Was there any audible sound?"

If you define audible sound simply as a disturbance creating waves of certain frequencies in a medium, the answer must be "Yes." Human experience with falling trees tells you that the crashing tree will create audible sound waves in the air whether or not there is someone present to detect them. On the other hand, many people agree with the U.S. Navy technicians who instruct their sonar operators that sound requires a source, a medium to transmit it, and a detector to hear it. If any one of these three requirements is missing, there can be no sound. If there is no detector, there is no sound. By this definition, the great expanses of oceans are soundless except where and when a sea creature or a man, dipping his hydrophones, eavesdrops on the denizens of the sea.

There is also another debatable question: where is the sound you hear? It is certainly not where the sound is created, since physically, you are not at the place where the impact started the vibrations. It is not at your outer ear; that merely serves as a kind of reverse trumpet, funneling in the sound waves. You hear sound within your brain, and by the time you do this, the sound is no longer a wave passing through a medium. The energy in the wave has been changed into electrical impulses. The effect of electrical impulses on your brain is what you have come to know as sound. For you, and for everyone else, all sound is within the individual's brain.

Energy carried by the sound wave travels only about an inch from your outer ear before it is transformed into electrical energy. In that distance, it travels through air, liquid, and solid matter—the bones of your skull. The energy carried by the sound wave is reduced, but its effective pressure is increased, and, finally, the energy of the sound is changed into electricity. All this occurs in the split second that elapses between the time the sound wave enters the outer ear and the time the brain is aware of the sound.

When Thomas Edison built the first phonograph in 1877, he used the principle of the human ear to record sound, and reversed the process to reproduce the sound. He did not follow the lead of earlier inventors who had tried to make "talking machines" by imitating the action of the human speech organs (see page 58), but rather built on the work of Alexander Graham Bell who had invented the telephone the year before. Since Bell was a teacher of the deaf, it was natural for him to use the human ear as a model. And ever since, from the first wax cylinder that captured a scratchy "Mary had a little lamb" in Edison's laboratory in Menlo Park, New Jersey, to the latest stereo tape or record of rock or Beethoven, the mechanical reproduction of sound has been based on a simplified version of the ear.

A person's first contact with a sound is the outer ear; it serves to gather the sound waves. In a recording machine, the microphone serves the same purpose. Microphones can gather in sound waves either from one direction—*unidirectional*—or from all directions—*omnidirectional*.

Omnidirectional microphones are fine when you wish to record everything that is going on around you, or if you wish to record a musical group. But there are times when a unidirectional microphone is very useful. Have you ever listened to someone talking over a public address system and found that his voice was almost drowned out by squeals and howls from the loudspeakers? That noise is called *feedback*. The microphone is picking up the sound of the person's voice as it comes out of the loud speakers and feeding it back over and over again into the microphone. A unidirectional microphone, aimed at the person's mouth, does not pick up as much feedback from the loudspeakers, and so the unwanted noise is kept to a minimum.

Man's rather flat outer ears are omnidirectional. The two ears, placed on opposite sides of the head, produce the *stereophonic effect* (as opposed to *monaural*—one-eared) which we regard as natural sound. Located close to the skull, his ears are less efficient sound funnels than the ears of many animals. Mammals whose lives depend on *flight* rather than *fight* often are equipped with outer ears that are large in proportion to their heads. The rabbit is probably the best known example, but if you look at such animals as the jerboa (desert mouse), the giraffe, and the deer, you will see that their ears also are very large for the sizes of their heads.

Most animals' ears have another advantage over those of

man. A few people can "wiggle" their ears, but most people must move their entire heads in order to move their ears. Even those who learn to wiggle their ears do not improve their hearing as a result. Many animals, however, can move their ears somewhat like directional antennas. This probably is of help in determining the direction from which a sound originates. The front, or open end, of the ears funnel in the sounds which concern the animals, while the backs of the ears partially screen out other sounds. Thus, their ears can function somewhat like unidirectional microphones in picking up mainly the desired sound.

Lacking the ability to wiggle his ears, the human must depend entirely on the placement of his ears for locating the origins of sounds. A sound that is created equidistant from each ear is received simultaneously by both ears and they relay it simultaneously to the brain. If the sound arrives a little later at the left ear, it reaches the brain a little later than sound from the right ear. The brain recognizes that the source of the sound must lie to the right since the sound had to travel farther before it reached the left ear. Moreover, the hard, flesh-covered skull absorbs and reflects some of the sound. The head creates a sound shadow. When the sound arrives at the left, or shadowed, ear, it is slightly less intense. This shadowing effect is particularly noticeable in sound waves with frequencies above 3,000 cps (3 kHz).

The less intense the sound, and the longer the interval between the arrival of the impulses from the two ears, the farther to the right the sound originated. The longest interval and the greatest shadowing occur when the source of the sound is on a line with the right ear. The change in intensity is not very great, and the distance around the head from one ear to the other is less than 1 foot. When you recall that the sound probably is traveling at more than 1,100 feet per second, the ability of the brain to recognize the very minute time intervals and differences in intensity is amazing.

The effect of the time interval and the difference in intensity on the location of sound can be demonstrated. Earplugs or earphones are fitted to each ear and attached to a computer which sends independent sound impulses at selected intervals and intensities to each ear. Although all of the sounds originate at the earplugs or earphones, as the intervals and intensities are changed, the brain interprets the sounds as originating directly behind the head or even inside the head. The computer can be programed so that the source of the sound seems to be moving slowly in an arc around the inside of the back of the skull from one ear to the other.

YOU CAN PROVE, without using a computer and wired earplugs or earphones, that you need two ears to figure out where a sound originates. Close your eyes and have someone clap his hands as he moves about the room silently. Try to locate the origin of each sound. Then repeat the experiment with sound blocked out of one ear. You can use an earplug, such as the kind used for swimming, or just hold your hand tightly over one ear. Compare the times you correctly locate the source of the sound with one and with both ears.

Research at the Bell Telephone Laboratories has shown that, in addition to using two ears, a listener must move his head slightly to insure achieving the stereophonic effect. A visitor, accidentally entering the laboratory of one of the researchers, Dr. Robert Hanson, in 1960, would have had good cause to believe that either he or the scientist had lost his reason. The visitor would have been confronted by a two-headed wonder—the dignified head of Dr. Hanson, white hair, eyeglasses, and all, surmounted by the head of a handsome young man. The freak was intently listening to

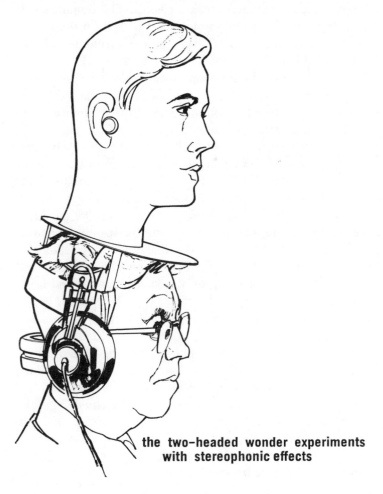

the two–headed wonder experiments
with stereophonic effects

137

music from a hi-fi. On closer examination, the upper head would prove to be a model that might more often be found atop a dummy in a clothing store display window.

Dr. Hanson's ears were covered with large muff-like earphones that eliminated outside sounds. The dummy's ears each contained a microphone which picked up the sounds of the music and relayed them to the earphones on Dr. Hanson's head. The music, as heard by Dr. Hanson, had the desired stereophonic effect. However, when the scientist removed the model's head and placed it on the table, the music relayed to his earphones lacked the feeling of depth that is characteristic of the stereophonic effect. As long as the dummy's head was attached to his, it moved whenever his head moved, thus picking up the sound of the music from various angles. But when Dr. Hanson removed the dummy's head and placed it on the table, there no longer was any movement of the microphones, and the music received by Dr. Hanson lacked auditory perspective. The tiny movements which we constantly make with our heads play an important part in determining what we hear. These same head movements also help us decide whether a sound originates above or below, and in front of or behind our heads.

The human outer ear serves more than one purpose. The outer ear protects the delicate mechanism within just as the hard outer shell of the microphone cushions it against hard knocks, water, and dirt. The outer ear does all this and even more to protect the delicate *eardrum* that lies only about 1 inch from the entrance to the *ear canal*. The eardrum is a very thin membrane sometimes called the tympanic membrane. It is about 0.1 mm thick—about as thick as a sheet of notebook paper—and has a total area of about 1 square centimeter. The eardrum must be flexible enough to vibrate in response to sound waves of many different frequencies and intensities. But eardrums can lose their flexibility rapidly when the temperature and moisture conditions change slightly.

the area of the human eardrum is about 1 square centimeter

Even with such a very sensitive membrane, you can go out in weather that may be more than 70° F colder than the house temperature which you just left without noticing any change in your ability to hear. The inch-long canal forms a snug little pocket in which the temperature and humidity around the eardrum are practically unchanged in spite of what happens to the environment around the outer ear.

Sound waves moving into the outer ear are amplified as they pass through the ear canal. The canal acts much like an organ pipe to increase the intensity of the sound. Sound waves between the frequency of 3,000 cps and 4,000 cps may be intensified as much as 4 times as they pass through the canal. Other frequencies are less affected.

The vibrating sound waves push against the eardrum as they reach the end of the ear canal. The force required to set the eardrum in motion is very small. It is, in fact, so small that it is measured in *dynes*. One dyne is the amount of force, push or pull, that, when applied for 1 second to 1 gram of matter (less than $\frac{4}{100}$ ounce) changes the speed of that matter so that it moves 1 centimeter faster or 1 centimeter slower in 1 second. Suppose an object that weighs 1 gram is moving at a speed of 25 centimeters per second. If you push it onward with a force of 1 dyne for 1 second, it would move 26 centimeters per second from then on. If you pulled it back with a force of 1 dyne, it would move forward at only 24 centimeters per second from then on. As another example of how small a force a dyne is, imagine how many dynes are needed to overcome the force of gravity pulling on 1 ounce of cheese or any other substance. If you were to hold up an ounce of cheese, you would have to use 28,000 dynes of upward force to overcome the pull of gravity. When you hold 1 pound of cheese in your hand, you are exerting a force of 448,000 dynes. But $\frac{2}{10000}$ of a dyne is enough to move an eardrum $\frac{1}{1,000,000,000}$ (one billionth) of a centimeter. This slight movement occurs when the least sound most people can hear reaches the eardrum; it is the threshold of hearing for most people, and the sound is 0 decibels. When a noise is so loud that it causes pain and can result in damage, when it is 140 db, the movement of the eardrum is only about $\frac{1}{1000}$ (one thousandth) of a centimeter.

The eardrum corresponds to the diaphragm in a microphone and in a telephone transmitter. Even though these diaphragms are made of thin discs of metal and the eardrum is a living membrane, both can be made to vibrate by sound waves whose force is measured in dynes. All the many different kinds of microphones that are in use today depend on a diaphragm that can be set in vibration by a force as tiny as a small fraction of a dyne.

In a telephone transmitter, sound waves from the voice set the diaphragm in motion. The vibrating diaphragm squeezes carbon particles together and then releases them as the diaphragm vibrates. This movement of the carbon particles causes fluctuations in a weak electric current that

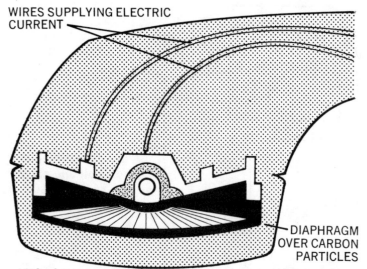

WIRES SUPPLYING ELECTRIC
CURRENT

DIAPHRAGM
OVER CARBON
PARTICLES

a telephone transmitter uses the energy of sound waves to alter an electrical current

is always flowing through them. The fluctuating electrical impulses are then sent by wires and relays to the telephone receiver at the other end.

In a dynamic microphone such as is commonly used for tape recorders or public address systems, the transducer consists of a small coil attached to the inside of the diaphragm. This coil moves back and forth between the poles of a magnet as the diaphragm vibrates. The movement between the poles changes the energy of motion of the sound waves into electrical impulses that are transmitted by wires. There are at least five other common kinds of microphone transducers, including one which uses carbon granules like the telephone transmitter.

The transducer in the human ear is the *cochlea,* but unlike the transmission in a microphone, the vibration from

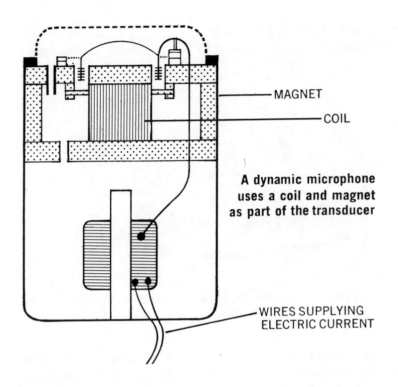

MAGNET

COIL

A dynamic microphone uses a coil and magnet as part of the transducer

WIRES SUPPLYING ELECTRIC CURRENT

the eardrum must be relayed before reaching it. Attached to the inside of the eardrum is a tiny bone called the *hammer* (*maleus*). The hammer is one of three small bones that make up the moving parts of the middle ear, which occupies a cavity in the skull. The handle of the hammer covers about one half of the eardrum and it is rigidly attached. Every motion of the eardrum moves the hammer. Every motion of the hammer, in turn, moves the *anvil* (*incus*), the tiniest bone in the human body. And each vibration of the anvil vibrates the third bone, the *stirrup* (*stapes*). The stirrup is attached to the *oval window* which forms the entrance of the *inner ear*.

The three tiny bones, hammer, anvil, and stirrup, are suspended in the middle ear's cavity and are surrounded by air. When the air pressure inside the cavity and the air pressure around you are the same, you do not feel anything unusual. But air pressure on the outside of the eardrum changes frequently. When you drive up a steep hill or mountain, or even when you ride in an elevator to the top of a tall building, you move from a place where the air pressure is greater to a place where the pressure is somewhat less. Even though the change in pressure may not be very much, your flexible eardrums are aware of the difference. The pressure of the air inside the cavity of the middle ear is greater than the pressure outside, and your eardrum bulges slightly outward. Your hearing is dulled or blurred, and if the change is too great, you feel pain. In cases of extreme

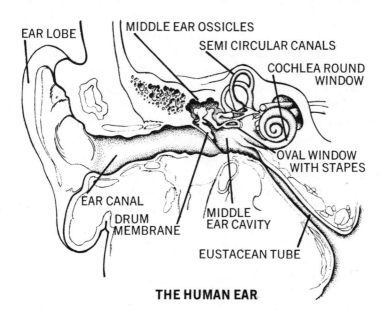

THE HUMAN EAR

pressure differences, it is possible to break the eardrum.

When you come down from a great height, or when you dive into deep water, the reverse occurs; your eardrum is bulged inward with the same uncomfortable results. Most people have learned that the solution of this discomfort is to "pop" their ears by yawning or swallowing hard. Such an action opens momentarily the tiny *eustachian tube* which runs from each middle ear cavity to the *pharynx*—the cavity at the back of the mouth. In this way, the air in the middle ear cavity comes into contact with the outside air, and the pressure is equalized on each side of the eardrum, allowing it to resume its normal shape.

The bones of the inner ear improve our hearing ability in two ways. First, the bones act like a lever and increase the force exerted by the sound waves on the eardrum. You know how to use a lever to lift a heavy stone. If you tried to lift the stone straight up, you probably could not budge it, but by applying a small force at the end of the lever, you can exert enough force on the stone to raise it off the ground. The smaller force working over a greater distance exerts a greater force through a smaller distance.

Similarly, the distance the vibrating eardrum moves the handle of the hammer bone in the middle ear is far greater than the distance the part of the stirrup attached to the oval window is moved. As a result, the force on the oval window is greater.

The second way the force on the oval window is increased has to do with its size. Because the area of the oval window is only about $\frac{1}{25}$th the area of the eardrum, the force transmitted to it is concentrated on a smaller area. The combined effect of these two mechanical means of increasing the force exerted by sound waves allows us to hear many sounds which we would otherwise miss. Without the middle ear to intensify sound, our threshold of hearing would be about 30 db instead of 0 db. This means that, because of the action of the middle ear, we can hear sounds that are 1,000 times weaker.

On the other side of the oval window lies the inner ear, which is really a system of small cavities in the bone of the

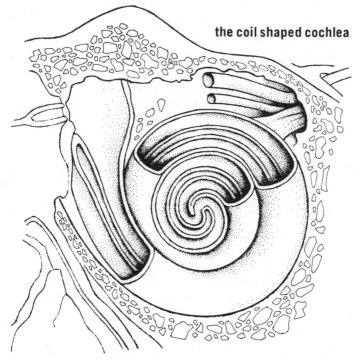

the coil shaped cochlea

skull. The first of these cavities is the cochlea—the transducer. This is coil-shaped, like the shell of a snail. If you could straighten the cochlea out, it would have the shape of a windsock.

145

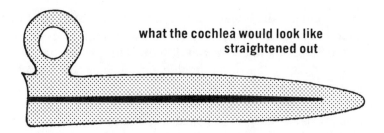

what the cochlea would look like
straightened out

Along the middle of the cochlea there is a partition. At the wide end, there are two windows. One is the oval window to which the stirrup bone of the middle ear is attached; the other is a round window which is separated from the middle ear by a membrane. The cochlea contains three canals or ducts, filled with a liquid that is about twice as thick (viscous) as water. Vibrations of the oval window set the fluid in motion, which in turn, starts the partition vibrating.

The motion energy of the vibrations is changed into electrical energy in the *organ of Corti* that lies on the *basilar membrane* which makes up the base of the cochlear canal. The most important parts of the organ of Corti are its approximately 23,500 hair cells and the nerve fibers from the auditory nerve, which extend into the organ of Corti and connect with the hair cells. As the basilar membrane vibrates in response to sound waves, the hair cells bend. This stimulates the nerve fiber endings and produces the electrical impulses that the auditory nerve carries to the brain. It is these impulses which the brain interprets as sound.

Man's knowledge about the workings of the inner ear was limited for a long time by its location within the skull. A cochlea removed for examination is no longer a living, reacting cochlea. Exposed to air, the hair cells collapse, shrink, and lose the ability to react. The scientist can examine it and propose theories about how it works, but he cannot actually see it in operation. Dr. Georg von Békésy changed that.

Dr. von Békésy was born in Budapest, Hungary, graduated from the university there, and went to work as a physicist for the Hungarian Telephone System. When the Communists took over power in his native country, Dr. von Békésy moved first to Sweden, and, in 1949, to the United States, where he taught at Harvard University. There, he conceived and carried out the experiment in which, for the first time, he exposed a working cochlea. Working on a cadaver, he bored a hole through the skull bone and through the cochlea until the basilar membrane was uncovered. He added a salt containing aluminum and coal particles to the jelly-like fluid inside the cochlear canal. These particles made movement within the fluid visible. Then, using stroboscopic light and a microscope, he proceeded to watch the effect of sound waves on the basilar membrane and the organ of Corti. Later, he made models of the cochlea, and did much of his research on the models. Because of these experiments, in 1961, he was the first physicist to win the Nobel Prize in medicine.

Until von Békésy's experiments, it was generally believed that fibers within the basilar membrane vibrated in response to different frequencies. It was assumed that shorter fibers, like shorter strings on a piano, vibrated to high frequencies while longer fibers responded to the lower frequencies. Today, we know that the whole membrane responds, but that the area of maximum response varies with the frequency. The entire membrane does not vibrate equally all along its length. Vibrations that result from high-frequency

147

sounds are strongest near the oval window. As the frequency becomes lower, the strongest vibrations occur nearer the other end of the membrane. This knowledge has led to a theory that can explain the fact that most people lose their hearing sensitivity for high frequencies before they lose it for the lower frequencies.

It is known that as people grow older, they usually first begin to have difficulty hearing such high-frequency spoken sounds as *f, s, th, ch,* and *sh*. The sentence "They had to stand in church," sounds like "ey had to tand in ur." If the listener knows the subject under discussion, his brain tends to fill in the blanks, and he understands the statement. But if he hears the sentence without any previous preparation, he may suspect that the speaker is mumbling and may ask him to repeat the statement, or to speak more clearly.

One explanation of this selective loss of hearing is based on von Békésy's discoveries about the effect of vibrations on the basilar membrane. High-frequency sounds have their maximum effect at the beginning of the membrane. Lower frequencies must also pass through this portion. The greatest pressure from excess noise occurs at the beginning of the membrane and so that is the first to lose its sensitivity. A more common explanation is that the tiny bones in the middle ear move less freely with the passing years and so are less able to transmit high-frequency vibrations. Whatever the reason for loss of hearing with age, one thing is certain: excessive noise can result in loss of hearing sensitivity, and even, in some cases, in deafness at any age.

In the past, men who worked in noisy places, such as boiler factories, expected to lose their hearing. Aware of the problem, many industries have adopted special measures to protect their workers, and they insist that these be used whether the worker agrees or not. The men who work around the big jet airplanes as they prepare to take off or as they taxi into the terminals must wear huge muff-like ear coverings. The drivers of racing cars also must protect their ears from the roar of the revved-up engines.

Earmuffs and earplugs are not the only modern approach to noise control in industry. Where possible, new buildings which are to house noisy machinery can be located on a hilltop rather than in a valley. Sound waves tend to be deflected upward, and so, move off from the hill rather than remaining concentrated within the bowl of the valley. Even the prevailing winds can play a part. Sound waves, traveling into the wind, are deflected upward away from the ground and people, while those that move with the wind are deflected downward toward the ground. With this in mind, buildings can be planned so that noisy operations are kept upwind, away from the rest of the plant. Acoustical materials can be used to absorb some of the sounds, and, in some cases, less noisy machinery can be chosen. For example, the common air compressor used in constructing high-rise buildings operates at 110 db, but quieter, more expensive models are available.

Even with all the knowledge we now have, and in spite of many attempts on the part of industry to protect employees, we still have a long way to go. At the National Council on Noise Abatement symposiums, held in February, 1969, it was estimated that about 6 million employees work under conditions that are dangerous to their hearing.

The noise pollution problem is not limited to industrial workers. Dentists, with their powerful, whining drills, have been found to have an exceptionally high hearing loss. People walking on noisy streets; women working in kitchens with automatic dishwashers, mixers, and blenders; families living under the takeoff and landing patterns of airports are only a few of those whose hearing and general health are beginning to suffer from the excessive noise in the environment. Eleven French towns around Orly airport outside of Paris sued three airlines to force them to pay for sound-proofing seventeen schools and five hospitals. And, in 1971, the Los Angeles City government bought 1,994 houses in the vicinity of a new airport runway, and relocated about 8,000 people at a total cost of more than $200,000,000.

In Knoxville, Tennessee, Dr. David M. Lipscomb, a researcher at the University of Tennessee, collected some tape recordings of rock music at a local discothéque. These tapes showed that the decibel rating of the music played was about 120. For three months, he treated a guinea pig to these tapes, at about the same intervals of time that a regular patron of the discotheque might be expected to listen to its music. There is no report on how well the guinea pig enjoyed the music, but at the end of the three months, microscopic examination showed that some of the cells of its cochlea had been destroyed. The damage resulted not from the style of music, but from the intensity and the fact that the tape constantly repeated the exact same frequencies. Rock music, played at a more reasonable decibel level and with a normal amount of variation in the tape recordings and, therefore, the frequencies, is, of course, no more dangerous than any other style of music.

One conclusion can be drawn from all the studies of noise-pollution problems, whether they relate to jet airports, metal-stamping machines in factories, or rock music in a discothéque: to protect hearing is a problem of preventive medicine, since there is no cure for hearing damage once it has been done.

Sonic Booms
10

A force like the hand of an invisible giant pushed against the glass, metal window frames, and masonry of the buildings. The glass, like all glass, was brittle; it could not bend under the great pressure and then recover its shape. Two hundred windows crashed, splintered, and tinkled down to the floors of the buildings of the United States Air Force Academy at Colorado Springs, Colorado. Before the startled officers and cadets could react, the four F 105 Thunderchiefs of the U.S. Air Force had already passed over the nearby peaks of the mountains that cradle the Academy.

It could have been the opening scene of a spy movie with the enemy stealing U.S. planes to bomb the Academy. It was, in fact, U.S. pilots flying low over the buildings as part of the dedication service of a new Academy display. Because the lead plane was flying faster than sound, it trailed a cone of highly pressurized air. The ground side of the base of the cone touched down just as it reached the Academy buildings. The resulting sonic boom left behind piles of broken glass and some very red faces.

The entire outside of an airplane creates pressure waves as it pushes through the air, and so contributes to the total sound we hear when a plane flies above. However, most of

151

the sound results from the nose and tail of the plane compressing the air as the plane pushes forward. All the sound waves created by a plane moving at *subsonic* speeds (less than the speed of sound) are like sound waves from any other source; they spread outward in all directions like a giant expanding balloon. But when the plane moves at *supersonic* speeds (faster than the forward-moving waves), the balloon shape is distorted; one major cone extends outward from the nose of the plane and another from its tail.

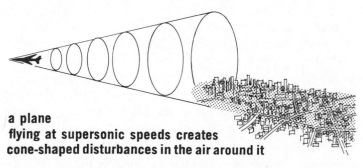

**a plane
flying at supersonic speeds creates
cone-shaped disturbances in the air around it**

It would seem that every plane traveling at supersonic speeds above land areas would leave behind it a trail of destruction. Fortunately, for mankind in a hurry, it does not happen quite this way. The energy in the pressure waves of each cone, like the energy in the pressure waves created by your voice, become less concentrated as the waves move outward. The farther the listener is from you, the less energy from your voice reaches and vibrates his eardrums. Similarly, the farther the plane is from the ground, the less damage the cones create, providing all other factors are equal.

However, all other factors are rarely equal. Sound waves are bent by temperature changes in the medium through which they are passing. The layers of air closest to the earth show the greatest temperature variations. Even within short distances, there may be considerable temperature variation. Perhaps you have noticed sometimes that as you walked along a road the air felt cooler in one place than in another. These kinds of temperature variations can affect sound waves in somewhat the same way that lenses focus the heat rays from the sun. The concentration of energy may be sufficient to cause the sonic boom to break windows in one place, while a few hundred feet away, the boom may be no more than a startling noise.

Ever since the first sonic boom shook the earth, there have been conflicting reports about the damage created by these sounds. At first, the booms were regarded as playthings by stunt pilots. They learned that their normally subsonic flights could be made momentarily supersonic by taking advantage of gravity. They dived at full power, creating booms like the sound of a cannon. This became a favorite closing act at the air shows that were popular in the early 1950s. However, when a practice run of this type damaged the floors and doors of an airport, the stunt lost its popularity.

As the U.S. Air Force added supersonic planes, complaints about sonic booms began to pour in. The Air Force values its supersonic planes, and in the beginning, was fearful that reports of damage might lead to the banning of such planes. Therefore, it is understandable that the Air Force was not very pleased with publicity about sonic damage. There was a suspicion that some reports of sonic damage were exaggerated, sometimes to make a good story better and sometimes to make a profit by suing for damages. The Air Force conducted many tests of the effects of sonic booms on people, animals, and buildings. They also investigated every claim for damage from sonic booms. In some cases, their suspicions proved correct, but they found enough evidence of real damage to order pilots not to fly at supersonic speeds above populated areas.

About 240 miles southwest of the Air Force Academy is the Four Corners where Colorado, New Mexico, Arizona, and Utah join together. By any definition, this would not be considered a highly populated area. If you were to draw a circle with the center at the Four Corners and a radius of 75 miles, you would include only four towns with populations over 2,500. Durango, the largest, has only a little over 10,000—about as many people as live in a single apartment complex in New York City. For the most part, the homes of the people who try to earn a living from this barren land are widely scattered. Yet, sonic booms in this section are of great concern.

Two or three hundred years before Columbus came to America, an Indian tribe, the Anasazi (a Navajo word meaning "Old Ones"), moved into huge, shallow caves that lined the sides of the deep canyons. Their cliffside houses were outstanding examples of engineering and masonry-building skills. They might be called America's first apartment houses. One of these houses, known today as Cliff Palace, has over 200 rooms for daily living and 23 ceremonial rooms. For some reason, perhaps continuous drought, the Anasazi abandoned these homes about 700 years ago. The same dry climate that may have driven the people away has preserved many of the houses and the things that the Anasazi left behind.

These early Americans had no written history. Even their legends disappeared as they became absorbed, probably by the Pueblo tribes that had wandered into the Southwest. Only the abandoned homes of the Anasazi stand as monuments to their great past and as clues to their daily lives. Archeologists, digging carefully with hand tools and pushing aside dry dust with soft brushes are slowly returning the "Old Ones" to their place in history. But what the centuries of dry climate have preserved, high-flying planes are destroying.

On August 11, 1966, a Navajo Indian gazed upward at a house that had stood secure for hundreds of years in the shadow of a cliff in secluded Canyon del Muerto, part of the Canyon de Chelly National Monument. High above, invisible to the Navajo, a military jet plane roared past on a routine flight. A boom of ear-aching intensity shook the boxed-in canyon, and as the man watched, the sandstone cliff began to crumble. Slowly at first, and then gathering speed, the face of the cliff disintegrated with a roar. The falling sandstone crunched downward on the ancient dwelling. When quiet returned to the canyon and the dust finally settled, the cliff house had disappeared forever, and with it went the historical clues which it might have revealed.

If this one dramatic event were the whole story, it would be a great loss indeed, but unfortunately, there is much more damage involved. Far more important to the national parks and national monuments of the western deserts are the small but frequent catastrophes which are often described as *noise erosion*. The 75-mile circle around the Four Corners contains two of the finest cliff-dwelling sites, Mesa Verde National Park in Colorado and Canyon de Chelly National Monument in Arizona. A somewhat larger circle, with a radius of about 200 miles, includes nearly all of the major cliff-dwelling sites in the United States. A plane flying at Mach 1, the speed of sound, could cross such a circle in about sixteen minutes. At Mach 2, twice the speed of sound, it would take only half as long. If supersonic transport (SST) planes, traveling as fast as 1,800 miles per hour, are ever used in cross-country flights, a SST pilot could pass over the historic circle almost before he was aware that he had reached it.

By 1970, the pueblos and cliff houses of Canyon de Chelly, a 35-mile long and 1,000-foot deep slit in the desert's surface, were shaken not once or twice, but well over 100 times each year. The chief ranger expressed his concern and reported that some booms are powerful enough to shake open the door of the rangers' station. The situation is also serious at Montezuma's Castle National Monument, a 700-year old pueblo. One employee of that monument said that each time a sonic boom touches down, "I run out to see if it is still here."

Most people are in a hurry, and so it was inevitable that the faster-than-sound military planes would lead to similar faster-than-sound commercial planes. At about the same time that plans for the SST's were appearing on the drawing boards of the airplane manufacturers, protests were being organized around the world. Delegates to a noise abatement conference in London were met by pickets carrying signs reading, "No Noise Is Good Noise." In Washington, a group of scientists released a study made at the suggestion of the Secretary of the Interior. They estimated that regular commercial supersonic flights would expose 20 to 40 million Americans to from 5 to 50 sonic booms a day. At another conference in Paris, several countries, including Sweden, Switzerland, Norway, West Germany, and the Netherlands, said that they intend to ban supersonic overflights completely. For the first time, people were asking not "Is it safe for those who fly?" but "Is it safe for those on the ground?"

Whenever enough people become concerned, it is certain that a study will be made. A Long Island company developed a simulator that could test the effects of sonic booms on apartments. In California, two wooden houses were built with pressure instruments embeded in the walls to test the effects of the booms. Horses, cows, pigs, and even minks were studied to find their reactions to booms. People who were accustomed to hearing booms and people who rarely, if ever, had heard one were subjected to sonic booms, and their physiological responses were observed. When the tests were completed, some facts had been established, but there were still differences of opinion. The sonic boom of a plane flying at Mach 2 and at 60,000 feet (where most SSTs are expected to operate) could extend for about 25 to 40 miles on each side of its track, but usually only a few windowpanes are broken by sonic booms. Animals, other than birds, seem to ignore the booms. But people, injured or not, do not like sonic booms. However, some investigators are convinced that people can become used to booms and eventually hardly notice them. Others are equally convinced that people can never accept or ignore this noise.

The first model SST, the Concorde 002 developed by England and France, was tested over an 800-mile strip of England in September, 1970. Although one Scot sued the English government for 5s.6d (66¢) for glue to replace a ceiling tile shaken loose by the sonic boom, there seems to

157

have been little other damage. Noise meters, sheets to catch dust, strain gauges, and other devices to measure damage were installed in St. David's Cathedral in Pembrokeshire. There was no damage to the cathedral during this flight, but many people are concerned about the effect of repeated overflights on medieval cathedrals and other historical buildings.

In addition to ear-splitting sonic booms, the side noises of the SSTs on the runway at takeoff and landing are still unacceptable. And some scientists are concerned about the effect on the upper atmosphere of the water vapor, sulfur dioxide, and other pollutants given off by the planes.

There are three apparent alternative means of dealing with sonic booms: ignore the people; prohibit supersonic flights; find a way to eliminate the boom from supersonic flight. Of the three, the last seems the most attractive. Unfortunately, at this time, no one knows how it can be done. Scientists are not saying that it is impossible; scientists have achieved many "impossible" things in the past. But at present, a compromise seems to offer the best solution. The supersonic planes can be flown faster than sound over the oceans, but they must be flown at less than the speed of sound over the land. Furthermore, the side noises on the runway must be reduced, and the upper atmosphere must be kept free of pollution.

During one phase of the Arab-Israeli conflict, instead of reducing the sonic boom, the combatants intensified it. Syrian and Israeli planes engaged in a "war of the booms." The jet pilots, by maneuvering the planes at low altitudes, intensified the sonic booms by up to twenty times over each other's cities. The resulting noise cracked a great number of windows and startled the inhabitants. Thus, the noise was used as a weapon, and served to remind the people of each of the countries that the enemy planes might just as easily have been carrying and dropping bombs.

Using Sound
11

So far, the fish have not complained about the proposed overwater flights of supersonic planes. At least, they have not picketed any meetings. Nor is there any plan to furnish them with earmuffs such as those supplied to the elephants in Safari Park, Windsor, England. This way of blocking sound was employed because the noise of subsonic airplanes that use the nearby airport was disturbing the elephants.

Such lack of planning does not mean that fish cannot hear. Most fish have two hearing systems: the ears which do not have external openings and thin lines of tubes and pits which extend along each side of the body. These *lateral lines* are very sensitive to changes in pressure. Low-frequency sounds are picked up by the lateral lines. Fish with swim bladders (see page 74) can hear better than those without. The swim bladder, in some way not yet completely understood, acts like the human middle ear and transmits sound to inner ear labyrinths near the skull. Fish with these hearing mechanisms respond to higher frequencies.

Generally, fish seem limited to hearing much lower frequencies than those that man can hear, but some scientists believe fish have greater auditory sensitivity than humans.

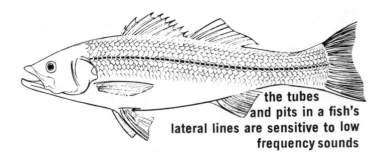

the tubes and pits in a fish's lateral lines are sensitive to low frequency sounds

One investigator found that salmon appear to be frightened by, or at least to dislike sounds with very low frequencies —from about 15 Hz to 300 Hz. When such sounds were produced in the water, the fish swam away as quickly as possible. He suggested that sonic alarms for salmons could be placed in rivers to guide them around hazards on their way to the spawning grounds.

The keen hearing of one kind of bird, the starling, led to a major tragedy. This common bird is generally not very well liked. It has a terrific appetite, eats a wide variety of foods, and chases away more desirable songbirds. At airports the starlings displayed a remarkable interest in one, and only one type of airplane, the Lockheed Electra, a turboprop plane. When a Lockheed Electra taxied out toward the runway, it would often be followed by a flock of starlings, searching the ground behind it. If the flight pattern required the plane to turn around before its takeoff run, the birds were sometimes sucked into the engines. This, naturally, interfered with engine performance, and the plane had to be called back and replaced. Unfortunately, on one occasion, a plane became airborne before the trouble was discovered, and sixty-two lives were lost in the resulting crash.

During the investigation that followed, the odd behavior

of the starlings was studied, revealing that one food on the starling menu is cricket. Crickets produce a high-pitched twitter by rubbing together the scrapers and files on the bases of their wings (see page 69). The noise of the turbo-prop engines of the Electra included a high-pitched whine. An analysis on an oscilloscope showed that the same wave frequencies were found in the twitters of a swarm of crickets and in the whine of the Electra. The starlings mistook the departing Electra for an abundant feast of crickets. Changing the sound of the engines saved the Electras from further unwanted attention by starlings.

Many insects can hear, but their hearing organs turn up in what seem to us odd places. The mosquito's hearing organs are at the bases of its antennae. The grasshopper has his on his abdomen, while the katydid and bee both have hearing organs on their legs. The katydid can hear sounds that are transmitted through the air, but not the bee—it can only receive sound from the vibrating structure on which it stands.

In their continuing fight to protect themselves from the insect hordes, men have used sound as a weapon. Recordings of the calls of female insects are made, and the sound is used to lure males of the same species into traps where they can be readily destroyed. Experiments at the Stored Products Research Laboratory in Savannah, Georgia, uncovered another use of sound as a weapon. When the female Indian meal moth is exposed to amplified sounds, most of its eggs do not hatch, and those few that do rarely live to become adults.

Men have also learned to use sound to change the behavior of animals in many ways. Newspaper stories about the effects of music on animals and plants appear quite frequently. It is not at all unusual to hear of a farmer who has wired his chicken house for sound, and then reports a substantial increase in eggs due to a certain song or a definite style of music. Other farmers have treated cows to serenades, and claimed increased milk output. It is interesting that the animals' and the farmer's tastes in music usually agree. Sometimes you may read of a farmer like the one in Normal, Illinois, who broadcasts songs to his cornfields. He claimed an increase of over twenty bushels per acre as a result of his corn concerts. Dr. George Milstein, a retired dentist and amateur gardener, has made a record of "Music to Grow Plants By." Dr. Milstein believes that high-pitched sound waves "cause the plants to keep their pores open longer and wider, allowing a greater exchange with the air around them." He insists that plants will grow faster if his record is played for them.

These tales may seem fantastic, but scientists have discovered that ultrasound can affect plant and animal growth. Just as audible sound can be pleasant and useful or unpleasant and harmful, ultrasound can either destroy or promote growth, depending on how it is employed. These effects of ultrasound are caused, in part, by the behavior of sound in water. Audible sound moves through water in approximately the same way it moves through air. Ultrasound, however, behaves differently in water. The very high-frequency ultrasound waves are very short. They travel only a short distance, but within that distance, they create a myriad of tiny bubbles. The formation of such bubbles in a liquid is called *cavitation*. As the bubbles collapse, they release energy in the form of pressure and heat. Depending on the intensity of the heat and the pressure impulses, material may react in different ways.

Properly controlled, cavitation bubbles can be employed to knock unwanted softer material from harder surfaces. This process is used in cleaning jewelry. An electronic generator supplies electrical energy to a transducer, usually located in the bottom of a small container holding water and a cleaning agent. The transducer sends ultrasonic waves through the liquid, forming cavitation bubbles. The jewelry to be cleaned is submerged in the liquid. As the bubbles collapse, the pressure impulses knock off the dirt, grease, and fine metal particles that cling to and dull the surface. When the machine is turned off, the jewelry emerges bright and shiny.

Many dentists today clean teeth with cavitation bubbles created by ultrasonic waves. Of course, a dentist usually cannot take your teeth out to submerge them in a container of liquid, so the liquid containing the bubbles is sprayed on your teeth. There, the collapsing bubbles knock the tartar off the harder enamel surfaces. The liquid with its bubbles can penetrate between the teeth and reach places that could not be cleaned by older methods. The process is not only quicker and more comfortable for you, but it also provides better protection for your teeth.

Ultrasonic cleaning is also used to prepare very fine wire when a completely smooth surface is needed. Very fine wire is made by drawing metal through a die of the desired dimension. Loose particles of metal will scratch the wire as it passes through the die. To prevent this, the die is submerged in a liquid that is subjected to ultrasonic sound waves. The bubbles knock all the loose particles from the wire and the die, and scratch-free wire is produced. The process is especially important in preparing wire used in the magnetic memories of computers. This wire is made of beryllium copper and is plated with a magnetic coat of nickel and iron. Even the slightest scratch in the magnetic coat can upset the functioning of the computer.

With the success of ultrasonic cleaners in industry, it was almost inevitable that some inventors would try to adopt the principle to household cleaning. Some of the earliest forecasts envisioned the day when ultrasonic transducers, strategically located throughout the house, would take care of all undesirable dirt. A more moderate suggestion was that these transducers might take over washing the dishes, especially the pots encrusted with burned food. In 1959, an ultrasonic dishwasher was produced. Unfortunately, its cost, $3,000 per dishwasher, made it impractical for most people. But pots are still being burned, and conventional dishwashers cannot scrub them, and so, the inventors are still trying. One company is producing an ultrasonic sink that uses sound waves of up to 40 kHz to scrub pans and dishes.

Experiences with ultrasonic cleaners have taught scientists and inventors that the very high frequency sound waves must be used with care. In cleaning metal, it is also possible to pit the surface badly unless the frequency and intensity are controlled. The cleaning agent added to the liquid must also be chosen with care since ultrasonic waves can cause chemical changes that are highly undesirable. For example, if ultrasonic sound is passed through carbon tetrachloride, a commonly used cleaner, the chemical breaks down and releases phosgene, a deadly gas that was used in poison gas attacks during World War I.

The ability to stimulate chemical change accounts for some of the unusual effects that ultrasonic waves create in living things. During World War I, Dr. Paul Langevin, a

French scientist, was experimenting with ultrasonic waves. When he tried passing them through the water of an aquarium, he found that the fish were killed instantly. An assistant who passed his hands through the path of the waves, jumped back in surprise. Although no mark appeared on his flesh, he felt an agonizing pain, as if his hand were being burned.

About three-fourths of a living cell is water. Ultrasonic waves passing through water behave in a similar manner whether the water is in a container, a single-celled organism such as a bacterium, the cell of a radish, the cell of a worm, or the cell of a man. If the intensity and frequency is right, cavitation bubbles are formed. Depending on the intensity, the ultrasonic waves may merely apply heat to muscles and joints, and thus, relieve pain and promote healing. They may, however, cause chemical changes to occur within the cells without disturbing the cell walls, or they may break down the cell walls as well as create chemical changes.

When only the heating effects are desired, ultrasound resembles diathermy treatments. If you have ever sprained an ankle or pulled a muscle while playing some sport, you probably know how heat helps relieve pain. Hot packs or a hot pad can make the injury much less painful. These heat sources only work near the surface. For deeper pains, diathermy or ultrasonic help is needed. Many college athletic departments and professional sports teams use ultrasound to relieve the pain of sports injuries such as charleyhorse and muscle spasms and to reduce swelling. A sprained ankle that ordinarily takes two to three weeks to heal can be treated with ultrasound and the player can be back on the team in less than three days.

The athletic trainers use the same machines doctors use

to ease the pain and inflammation of arthritis, bursitis, lumbago, and many other ailments. A transducer about the size of a flashlight is attached by a cable to an electrical oscillator. In the head of the transducer there is a quartz crystal that can be set to vibrate 1,000,000 times a second or more and produce ultrasound. The frequencies used for treating patients are between 800 kHz, and 1,000 kHz. The head of the transducer is bonded to the patient's skin with mineral oil or vaseline so that none of the ultrasound is wasted by leaking into the air. The transducer is kept moving across the patient's skin throughout the treatment which lasts from three to ten minutes, and the patient feels only a slight warmth in the area being treated. Ultrasound is considered very safe since there is a built-in safety valve: there can be no tissue destruction in the human body without first exceeding the physiological pain threshold.

When chemical changes without cell-wall destruction are produced by ultrasonic waves, some strange effects can be observed. A high-school student in Bergenfield, New Jersey, used ultrasonic waves to grow oversized radish plants. In an experiment prepared for a science fair, she exposed some radish plants to ultrasonic waves for twelve hours each day. Control radish plants, with all other conditions the same, were not exposed to the waves. After twenty-eight days, she found that the exposed plants were nearly twice the size of the control plants. Scientists working in laboratories with far more complex equipment have had similar results. Apparently, the chemical change that occurs within the cells exposed to ultrasonic waves results in accelerated growth.

If the intensity of the ultrasonic waves is great enough to break down the cell wall, the living cell is destroyed. For one-celled forms such as bacteria, this means total destruc-

167

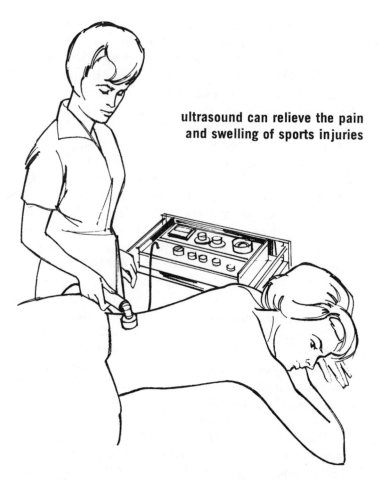

ultrasound can relieve the pain
and swelling of sports injuries

tion. This leads to the possibility of using ultrasonic waves
as a sterilizing agent. For more complex living things, such
as man, the waves can be pinpointed to a small area and
unwanted cells such as cancer cells can be destroyed.

Medical use of ultrasonic waves is not limited to their effects within cells. One company that was seeking to make a better paint sprayer discovered that ultrasonic waves could break the paint up into smaller droplets than the usual air-sprayers. This lead was picked up by doctors who found that by bombarding a cup of water with ultrasonic waves, they could produce a fog of droplets far smaller than those produced by steam devices. These droplets, only about $\frac{1}{1,000,000}$ of an inch in diameter, penetrated deep into the lungs of victims of some of the fatal lung diseases and gave at least temporary relief. About a year after this discovery, another doctor got the idea of using the superfine fog to vaccinate people against tuberculosis, a sometimes fatal lung disease that is especially common among the poor and deprived of the world. Instead of individual injections, children in groups were exposed for thirty minutes to an ultrasound-induced fog that contained both water droplets and live but harmless tuberculosis bacilli which they inhaled. If this process can be perfected, it may someday be possible to eliminate most of the old painful "shots" and instead have the patients spend a little time in a foggy room.

An ultrasonic scalpel that uses a frequency of 200 kHz for delicate surgery is another medical application of ultrasound. The scalpel can make cuts as small as $\frac{1}{1,000}$ of an inch, and so can cut smooth curves that would be impossible with ordinary instruments. Moreover, it can be adjusted so that it only cuts or so that it cuts and sears at the same time, thus stopping all bleeding as it operates.

New uses are constantly being devised for ultrasound. It can be used to detect tiny flaws in the thin enamel covering of a tooth so that early treatment can prevent cavities and tooth decay. It can be used as a sewing machine to bond two pieces of material without needle and thread. It can be used to massage the body, and thus relieve some of the tensions created by our noisy environment.

Man has come a long way in his use of sound from the animal-like grunts that probably proceeded human speech, through the jungle drumbeats that carry messages hundreds of miles, to tape recorders, and to modern medicine. Sometimes along the way, in his rush for new uses of sound, man has discarded older and sometimes better ways of doing things. For example, African tribes that once depended on drumbeats to send messages, now depend on the mails. Today, only very few of their members can understand or have the great skill required to send the drum messages.

True, drum messages could become confused if they were substituted for long-distance telephone calls over the 300 miles between Cleveland and Chicago, but there are parts of the world where this skill could still be used to great advantage. It is unfortunate that most people are impressed by mechanical inventions and do not recognize that the development of communication by drum required no less imagination and creativity than the development of the wireless or the telephone. If you doubt this, TRY INVENTING a language of drums with which you and your friends can communicate.

Man has learned to live in a world of sound and to use those sounds to reassure himself that all is well. One manufacturer designed a vacuum cleaner with plastic material that could muffle its roar. Marketing tests proved that it would not sell unless housewives were reeducated. Although the machine had the same cleaning power as its noisier cousins, women who used it claimed it did not do as good a job; they had come to associate the loud roar with a good job. In the same way, many people judge a car by the "solid" sound created by slamming a door, even though tests show that there is no relationship between the sound of the slamming door and the serviceability of the car.

What man has not learned is to live comfortably in a world without sound. David Humphreys, who led the expedition that found the northernmost tip of Greenland, said that the worst part of the journey was the silence of the frozen land. It was easier to adjust to the overwhelming cold and the days of unending darkness than to live in a world of perpetual silence.

Index